M000296968

Mrs. Eudora Holma
1925 Safari Dr.
Saint Joseph, MO 64506

SYMBOLISM IN THE GOSPEL OF JOHN

SYMBOLISM IN THE GOSPEL OF JOHN

Paul Diel

Jeannine Solotareff

Translated by Nelly Marans

1817

Harper & Row, Publishers, San Francisco

Cambridge, Hagerstown, New York, Philadelphia, Washington
London, Mexico City, São Paulo, Singapore, Sydney

Originally published in French by Payot, Paris, in 1983 under the title LE SYM-BOLISME DANS L'EVANGILE DE JEAN.

FIRST HARPER & ROW EDITION

Library of Congress Cataloging-in-Publication Data

Diel, Paul, 1893–
  Symbolism in the Gospel of John.

  Translation of: Le symbolisme dans l'Evangile de Jean.
  1. Bible. N.T. John—Criticism, interpretation, etc. 2. Symbolism in the Bible. I. Solotareff, Jeannine. II. Title
BS2615.2.D5413 1988   226'.5064   87-46204
ISBN 0-86683-509-1

---

88 89 90 91 92 HC 10 9 8 7 6 5 4 3 2 1

CONTENTS

Foreword

This work is based on manuscripts written by Paul Diel more than forty years ago. He was then discovering the close—and at first sight surprising—connection between what must be called the psychological pre-science of the symbolism of myths and the *science* of psychic functioning—the psychology of motivation—rooted in a methodical introspection.

Paul Diel was able to show in the works he published subsequently, especially in his studies of Greek and biblical mythology, that mythical symbolism stemmed from an intuitive and imaged introspection, and that nothing but an introspective psychology would enable us to rediscover its significance conceptually. In times when mythical symbols were intuitively felt and understood, they had an evocative power arousing an emotion springing from the depths of the human psyche. A methodical nonspeculative conceptual understanding of the mythical message can awaken a similar emotion in the face of life's dimension and its meaning, summoned up by the images of mythical symbolism. Today these images are misunderstood and dogmatized or lumped with the fables deemed to be barely worthy of the infancy of mankind. To do that is to forget that these myths were the core of cultural communities that lasted for centuries.

On the basis of the psychological exegesis that Diel left us, it has been possible to undertake a thorough translation of the entire text of John's Gospel, verse by verse, thanks to Diel's well-tried and -tested introspective methodology in which he thoroughly trained his students. "Method knows it all," Paul Diel used to say. Once it had been established, thanks to the strength of its creator's genius for introspection, it had the potential to bring about all the subsequent developments and applications.

In order for the reader to have a full picture of the symbolic significance of the Gospel of John, we decided—with the agreement of Jane Diel and the publisher—to include in this book the text of the Prologue to the Gospel that had already been translated and published in Paul Diel's last book, *Symbolism in the Bible*.

I wish to thank my friends of the Psychology of Motivation group for their friendly critiques and their suggestions.

J. S.

CHAPTER 1

Introduction

It is now widely agreed that the Gospel of John is a symbolic work. Yet in spite of its recent acceptance of symbolism, theological exegesis could not accept what a rigorous approach to mythological images does actually imply. Such exegesis can use this approach only insofar as it does not lead to a questioning of the articles of faith and fundamental dogmas: the reality of God, the divinity of Jesus, and his miraculous resurrection. This reservation, caused by attachment to dogmatism, leads to a difficulty in facing the hidden meaning of symbolic images. Thus, for instance, the blind and the deaf described in the Gospels are not those who are blind to the meaning of life and deaf to their own conscience (the meaning that will be developed in this work), but those who do not recognize the divinity of the Son.

The purpose of this preliminary comment is only to point out, from the outset, the dividing line between a theological approach (even if it has been updated) and a methodical psychological approach.

Theological exegesis could not be grounded in the science of symbolism, based on the Psychology of Motivation, without running the risk of having to give up the dogmas it is meant to justify and maintain. Psychological exegesis would lose all scientific value if it did not remain totally free of any dogmatically imposed interpretation.

One question comes immediately to mind: why does the Evangelist—by using a symbolic language—hide the truth he wants to express, why does he not spell it out as clearly as possible?

Symbolic thought is just as precise in its specific formulation as conceptual formulation. Had the Evangelist been less deeply imbued with his truth, he could not have achieved symbolic precision and he would have been compelled to express himself with the help of the philosophical speculation that was flourishing in his time. Thanks to symbolic formulation, he was able to avoid the danger of all speculative imagination, of all uncontrolled intuition. It is this same danger that we must overcome today through the precise formulation suited to the scientific spirit: the truths of the inner life need a precise psychological formulation. The unfortunate thing is that, in the absence of a method of transposition, an imprecise and arbitrary interpretation has entered into the structure of the old truth and destroyed the symbolic precision on which it was founded. To be sure, such an attempt at inadequate transposition can be seen as a historical necessity. A reasoned criticism is not aimed at such a necessarily insufficient endeavor, but only at the dogmatization of the error, even if the latter remains historically explainable.

Between the precision of the symbol and the precision of the psychological formulation, there is a decisive difference. Symbolism is an expression of intuitive and analogical thought: it is intuitively referring to the unfathomable depths of life. Should one accept the symbol without transposition, without translation, as a logical expression, error is unavoidable. The symbol does not aim at a logical proof, but at an intuitive conviction which is faith: an unshakable trust in the lawful organization of the physical world and of life; something that is available to any mind that knows how "to see"; a far cry from a belief in unprovable things, which is always underlain with doubt. While symbolic expression is perfectly consistent in itself, it is expressed in an illogical form; in Greek mythology, for instance, the sphinx talks and Pegasus flies away from the beheaded corpse of Medusa.

The two forms of expression have their advantages and disadvantages. Symbolic thought has the great advantage of being able to compress into a single image truths that, in conceptual language, can only be expressed through lengthy explanations that risk being obscure because they are so complicated. Symbolic thought is thus perfectly adapted to the expression of the only truths it deals with; that is, those of the inner life and its complexity. A necessarily complex translation of these deep truths becomes indispensable when—due to the progress of intellectual thought—the ability to grasp illogical images declines. The miraculous façade of these images and their illogicality seem to lend credence to the concept of a divine and supernatural intervention in natural phenomena.

Since the façade is mistaken for a reality, all these symbolic expressions are misunderstood and their true dimensions are lost. When it comes to the truth about inner life, a purely logical thought aiming at the translation of symbolic images will necessarily fall into absurdity: God becomes a real person. The translation can only achieve its aim by letting psychological understanding take the lead.

The intention of the Evangelist himself is to lead the reader in search of the deep meaning underlying the seemingly miraculous narrative. The Evangelist, using symbolic language, seeks to awaken essential conviction; i.e., faith. He seeks to stress the truth offered, not to explain it. The very nature of symbolic language compels him to relate true facts about psychic phenomena in an illogical and seemingly miraculous form, even though, on the other hand, he does not, as we shall see, miss an opportunity to express his aversion for belief in actual miracle.

Such a contrast can thus only be a means used to make us understand that narratives that seem miraculous in appearance have a hidden meaning. The danger of misunderstanding remains; it can only be avoided through strong faith or the endeavor of translation. But the danger that a deep and therefore hard-to-grasp truth may be misunderstood can never be entirely avoided and cannot therefore be blamed on mythical expression. Translation itself could not entirely avoid this danger, which appears, not in the form of the images' enigmatic compression, but in that of the complexity of the explanation. The ancient formulation of the truth is thus not insufficient: it is complete in itself; rooted in emotion in the face of the unfathomable depth of life, it was meant for an era that was less intellectualized than ours.

The Evangelist would not have been capable of explaining the message of Jesus, psychologically, according to the laws of psychic workings, just as a man of our time would not be capable of composing a genuine myth. Belief replacing the mystery of life with a miracle is an essential danger at all times. In our scientific era, belief is more destructive than it has ever been. It is unworthy of the scientific era. Only an explanation able to go into the depths of the psyche and, in conformity with the demands of our time, capable of remaining at the same time precise and methodological, can restore the true significance of the so-called miracle and incorporate it into the emotion in the face of life's mystery.

Science and religiosity (which must be distinguished from the religions) are destined to unite and sustain each other.

The grossly illogical utterances concluding every teaching of the Gospel's Jesus are—as we shall show—a means to call man to look for the significance hidden behind the symbolism. The Son of Man could not express the truth he proposes if he sought to avoid anything that might shock the dogmatism of the Pharisees. But in the Gospel of John, whose hero expresses himself only in symbols, this danger is even greater, for the illogicality of the symbol, if it is taken literally, is in fact a mad blasphemy. In the Johannine Gospel, one is under the impression that Jesus is seeking not to allay the perplexity and indignation of the Pharisees, but, on the contrary, to exacerbate it. He cannot be aiming at insulting the Pharisees so as to show up their ignorance or to prove that he does not fear their hatred. His attitude must therefore have another meaning. Now the hero of the Gospel of John is neither in words nor in deeds the real and historical Jesus; the Gospel is a symbolic expression of the words and the character of the historical Jesus depicted in the Synoptic Gospels. The attitude of Jesus in John's Gospel is thus a symbolic means of expression used to stress on the one hand the heroic nature of the sanctified man who, even though he is so conciliatory in all his purely human relationships, does not give an inch even under the threat of death, when it comes to his essential Mission; and this attitude is, on the other hand, a means used to stress the irreconcilable contrast between symbolic expression and literal understanding. For the dead belief of the Pharisees, all that Jesus says and does, his whole attitude, seem senseless: for the true faith, the contrary is true; i.e., the attitude of the Pharisees becomes senseless. Since their attitude is rooted in the misunderstanding of Jesus' message, true faith implies going beyond appearances and grasping the hidden essential. Symbolic expression in its most extreme form and the perplexity of the Pharisees denouncing blasphemy are thus a means for the Evangelist to compel the reader to seek and understand the true meaning of what he wants to say and of what he can only express through symbolism. The Evangelist could not have foreseen that this means would be turned against him and become the cause of a new misunderstanding. He could not have foreseen that a time would come, more naive than that of the Pharisees denouncing blasphemy and madness because Jesus claimed to be the Son of God, when people would fall into a new dogmatization based on a literal interpretation: the reality of Jesus' divine filiation. But the Evangelist would surely have denounced blasphemy had he been able to see the interpretation given later on by the Church to the myth of Redemption.[1]

Dogmatic error is the consequence of misunderstanding the texts. Only when we accept the mystery of the existing world,* symbolized by God the Creator, can we understand Scripture. The veracity of Scripture does not lie in its being dictated by a real God, but in a deep meaning in its symbolism, the meaning of life, hidden behind the façade of all the myths.

Revelation itself is only a mythical truth. It is not the revelation of a real god given to his real son, but that given by the essential impulse† of that man called the Son of God, in conformity with a metaphor very common in the Middle East.

What this vital impulse reveals is the strength of the human spirit and its capacity for spiritualization and sublimation, it is the immutable lawfulness ruling all that lives, it is immanent justice (immanent to the psychic functioning), stipulating that man, whatever the external conditions of his life, can find joy in the harmonization of his desires.

It is the revelation to the man Jesus and through the man Jesus of the meaning of life that has become a certainty. God being a symbol, the expression "Son of God" being a symbol, the salvation achieved by the Son, man among men, is achieva-

---

*What Paul Diel calls *apparition* has been translated as "the appearance" (of the manifest world), or "the existing world." —Translator.

†The word(s) *élan* or *élan vital* are used by Paul Diel to express that all living beings—and therefore man—are animated by a mysterious force. The translators chose the English "vital impulse" or "impulse" to render the concept of *élan*. "Elan" would have led to confusion (with Bergson's *élan vital*). —Translator.

ble—within the possibilities of each and every human being—by all those whose vital impulse endeavors to be fulfilled. It is the message that the savior hero sought to give to men who, living as he did in a decadent world, found themselves in utter confusion.

The birth, evolution, and death of mythical thought are depicted in all their magnitude by Paul Diel in several of his books: *Symbolism in Greek Mythology*, *The God-Symbol*, and *Symbolism in the Bible*. It is not possible, in the framework of this book, to give a detailed account of Paul Diel's thought, scientifically and methodically established and developed in his basic work: *La Psychologie de la Motivation*.

However, a few words of explanation are indispensable before we undertake to read the Gospel in its conceptual translation. It is necessary to define mythical expression in general, its function and the method that makes it possible to penetrate its deep meaning, before we approach the specificity of the Christian myth.

A myth is the emotional and imaged answer of the human spirit* to the fundamental questions it poses about the origin and cause of the world, death and its mystery, life and its meaning.

All cultural communities were founded on a mythical vision—this is a historical fact. The answers provided by the myth are imaged and their underlying significance was intuitively understood by a community whose members could thus rally around symbolic images. We must realize that the answers to these questions were truly fundamental; they gave man the possibility of overcoming his anxiety in the face of the unfathomable mystery of existence, of calming the fear of death and sublimating it into love of life.

---

*The French *esprit* has been translated either by "mind" or "spirit" according to context. Diel defines it as the organizational aspect of matter. The concept is thus extended to the whole of nature instead of being restricted to man's thought. This definition is fundamental for the understanding of Diel's thought.

It would have been preferable to use "spirit" all the time (1) because the word "mind" is too extensive, covering at the same time psyche, spirit, and intellect, which are concepts that Diel clearly distinguishes; (2) "spirit" would link up better with "spiritualize," which, as defined by Diel is the fundamental function of the human spirit.

However, "spirit" has spiritualist connotations that are an inconvenience in a scientific text such as this is.

It is clear that the message of Jesus, as transmitted to us by the Evangelists, belongs to the metaphysical and ethical realms—the metaphysical viewpoint, in its deep symbolic meaning, is simply the awareness of the mystery of existence. It is particularly brought out in the Gospel of John.

Out of all the allegorical or symbolic episodes narrated in the Gospels, an ethical meaning emerges. We now have to determine what can be a symbolic metaphysics and an ethics rooted in bio-psychology, both being the real foundations of any mythology. If it is true that the characteristic of myth is a symbolic statement about the origin of the world and the meaning of life, the Gospel of John is to be seen as pure mythical expression. The translation of the Christian myth will therefore be really convincing only if it is part and parcel of the translation of the universal mythical message.

The origin of mythical symbolism is to be found in cosmic allegory, based on the observation of the stars.

The mythical era of farmers followed the animistic cultures of hunters and shepherds. Life, for a tiller of the soil, depended on the motions of the stars ruling over sowing and harvesting. The stars, whose importance in daily life could not be ignored, were raised to the rank of benevolent or malevolent deities. They fought among themselves to grant their help to man or to withhold it. But would man have been able to interpret the alternance of day and night as a struggle between good and evil if he had not observed within himself an endless struggle between his sublime intentions and his perverse ones? The former, like the sun, bring him warmth and light; the latter, like the night, plunge him into darkness and disorientation. For it to be true, this affirmation presupposes that human beings are capable of introspection. It is on the basis of this essential given of the human condition that we can understand both animistic and mythical thought, which are projections onto the outer world of the hopes and anxieties experienced by man in the face of the dangers of existence and the unfathomable mystery of life and death.

The animistic era exorcises danger and fear in the face of the unknown in the environment.

The mythical era sublimates fear and transforms it into faith in the lawfulness of the world and life.[2]

At the root of these two forms of explanation of the world, we find the projective phenomenon, the expression of intuitive introspection that is typical of human beings. The magical realism of the primitive era saw the outer world (stars, animals, and plants) as being actually animated with intentions toward man. With the evolution of thought, it became mythical symbolism using elements of the outer world to represent human intentions symbolically. By virtue of the freedom it acquired by transcending reality, it became capable of creating symbols that were still borrowed from the outer world but were freed from the givens of reality (a talking serpent, a winged serpent, a centaur that was both man and horse). From the outset, animism had the potential to develop all the givens of human intentionality and the conflicts with which it is fraught. Mythical symbolism took upon itself to enlarge the vision brought about by the human spirit's introspective capacity.

Myth uses the form of a heroic struggle to represent the struggle between good and evil, between the perverse and sublime intentions clashing in the human psyche, the arena where man's essential destiny is played out. Man's evil is simply his ancestral tendency to blind himself about his own self and about the meaning of life. The good that man can do to himself is to become lucid about the deep intentions that move him, with the sole purpose of harmonizing them and thus finding the satisfactions of materiality, sexuality, and spirituality that are biologically rooted in the desire to live.

The struggling hero is thus the man in whom the call to the essential task of elucidation is sufficiently powerful for his inner strength—diversified in qualities and personified by the deities— to enable him to attack in his inner self his own *perversion* symbolized by monsters, and his *perversity* symbolized by demons, both originating in his blindness about himself.

Being able to develop the meaning and scope of symbolism thus implies a knowledge of psychological functioning, since lucidity and blindness are consequences of psychic functions that can be defined with a high degree of precision.[3] Lucidity about oneself, about one's most hidden intentions, is an evolutionary demand assumed by the superconscious, which is an evolved form of animal instinctivity, capable of giving a meaningful direction to life; the superconscious imposes, for the greater satisfaction of the individual, a harmonious reunification of the material, sexual, and spiritual desires; as the creator of myth, it shows thereby its power of essential orientation; all evolutionary capacities, all certainties in the face of life's meaning are rooted in ethical superconsciousness. The purpose of this more-than-conscious process is to guide consciousness, since the latter is limited in its adjusting forecasts by its tendency to refer only to external reality. Consciousness is often subject to an obsessive control by the subconscious that is a state of blindness about the self, rooted in an excess of affectivity. It is opposed in all aspects to the enlightening knowledge of the superconscious.

Desires, stemming from the material, sexual, and spiritual drives, are valuated either by the affective subconscious process or by the evolutionary superconscious process. Since they are subconsciously determined, they tend to multiply in an anarchic way. Essential desire, the expression of the superconscious process, is opposed to the exalted multiplication of material, sexual, and pseudospiritual desires. Thus determined by a quest for satisfaction that can be meaningful (superconscious) or meaningless (subconscious), valuated desires—in other words, interior tensions, motives, that are the consequences of the valuation of the desires—remain only too often hidden and lead to perverse actions as opposed to the satisfaction demanded by the evolutionary impulse.

To be lucid means to unmask the false subconscious motivations so as to heal the psyche and enable it to find joy, symbolized by "Heaven" in the Christian myth, or by Nirvana in the Hindu myth.

The knowledge of psychic functioning is thus acquired introspectively and only thus, since no outer observation could lead us to sure conclusions about the deep intentions ruling inner deliberation.

How would it be possible to talk about a mythical message, be it pagan or Christian (who could doubt that the Gospel is one?), springing from the human soul, without having a quite precise knowledge of the peaks of the human soul? But how would it be possible to talk about the evangelical message—rejected in its genuine significance by the quasi-totality of mankind—without having a knowledge of the chasms of the human soul?

This desire to investigate the psyche is opposed by the generally accepted convention that introspection is fraught with morbidity. Now, lucid introspection, though it is intuitive, is a natural phenomenon. Jesus and Buddha were particularly lucid in their introspections. Introspection can become methodical when it is capable of finding all the analogical ties linking the whole of the superconscious and subconscious psychic manifestations and when it leads to the definition of laws governing the transformation of superconscious motives into subconscious motives and of subconscious motives into superconscious ones.

These laws are the following: the law of ambivalence (breakup of the psychic qualities into two contradictory poles) and the law of harmony defined by the evolutionary play of differentiation and integration of the whole being the lawfulness of the psychic functioning.

The preliminary condition for deciphering myths is therefore a rigorous knowledge—in the most minute details—not only of the psychic functions but also of their dynamics; i.e., of the laws governing their functioning and relationships.

If there were no such laws, any possibility of methodical translation of the symbolic thought in dreams[4] or myths,[5] any possibility of avoiding arbitrariness, would have to be excluded.

Precise and detailed knowledge of the psychic functioning, making it possible to throw a clear and consistent light on the enigma of myths, shows that they had from the outset the ability to express the functioning of the human psyche and its deliberating dynamics. Myth is therefore a pre-science of psychic functioning.

On the other hand, knowledge of deliberation and its fluctuations, insofar as it enables us to understand consistently the significance of myths, has been well established by the Psychology of Motivation.

Only verification through consistency would give absolute proof. Consistency is a condition for the scientific nature of a proposition.

Human beings find it difficult to achieve satisfaction, and this stems from the fact that the exalted desire for pleasures, connected with a no less exalted desire—though a contradictory one—to consider oneself as a perfect specimen, is more or less hidden in the heart of every individual. This universal phenomenon, called in Greek mythology the revolt of Prometheus, in Judaic mythology original sin, in Christian mythology satanic temptation, is called in the Psychology of Motivation *vanity*, in its deepest etymological meaning; i.e., void, absence of any genuine satisfaction.

Vanity, the pretension to "be all and have all," offers man fallacious promises, bringing him only disappointments at best, and psychosomatic symptoms—be they neurotic or psychotic—at worst, all being the consequences of imaginative exaltation. Vanity in all its forms (worries, resentments, anxieties, greed, hatred) is an *exalted* attachment to multiple desires. It is but a disguised fear of life, an oblivion of the unfathomable mystery of existence. It prevents man from grasping the essential dimension of life. Only emotion in the face of the mystery of organization, when it is powerful enough to blossom into a sublime love of life, is able to dissolve the exaggerated importance given to accidental satisfactions.

Only such an emotion can free man from the vain exaltation of desires. Man's unconditional and demented love for his vain self—even at the cost of his soul—is the cause of all the sufferings of mankind, be they individual or social.

The victorious hero of the Christian myth, like the victorious hero of the Greek myth of Perseus, was able, by mastering vanity and its consequences, to show mankind the way to salvation, as will be demonstrated further on.

Yet vanity is a satisfaction, for otherwise its seduction would not be so strongly felt by the human psyche. What is difficult here is to grasp that such a satisfaction is false, causing uncounted dissatisfactions leading to new expressions of vanity, the consequence of which is an aggravation of incurable sufferings.

The real problem of human beings is thus to learn to distinguish between the genuine satisfactions of the material, sexual, and spiritual drives and the satisfactions of the very same drives as exalted by vanity, a power that is a master of deceit, ceaselessly fueling subconscious distortion and rejecting superconscious truth.

Pathological imagination, the exaltation of the ego, causes all the illnesses of the mind: nervousness, neurosis, and psychosis.*

---

*Diel distinguishes three levels of mental disorder: *nervosité*, *névrose*, and *psychose*, which have been translated as "nervosity," "neurosis," and "psychosis." In addition, Diel diagnoses a form of mental illness never before diagnosed: banalization—a state

Desire, whether it be material, sexual, or spiritual, is condemned—as soon as it is under the sway of exalted imagination—by essential desire, and is turned into guilty and inhibiting anxiety†; this anxiety, psychic energy repressed in the subconscious, reappears in the guise of a symptom. We will have the opportunity to develop this further when studying the cures brought about by Jesus. Ambivalently to these forms of essential deficiency, of perversion of the vital impulse, the psyche can eliminate as radically as possible the essential desire and kill the incriminating process: the superconscious. It is then possible for man to satisfy his most exalted and meaningless desires. Thus does the individual protect himself against any guilty suffering, which is a consequence, in the nervous psyche, of the desires' exaltation, but at the same time he deprives himself of any possibility of inner joy. He dehumanizes himself, he becomes what myths call "dead in the soul" and what the Psychology of Motivation calls "banalized." Besides its material and sexual forms, banalization has another and extremely pernicious guise: conventionality of the spirit. This is blind attachment to ruling ideologies. The Pharisees who represent, in the Gospel, conventional banalization, dogmatically attached to the Law of Moses, would be the most vehement enemies of the Nazarene.

Nervousness and banalization, perversion and perversity are the two distortions of the human psyche. These inner dangers, depicted by all myths, are rooted in a common cause: vanity.

Blind to the truth, deaf to the truth, inhibited before the truth (paralytics), possessed by the demon of vanity, and dead in the soul, such are the people we meet in the world of the gospels.

Through the power of his word and his influence, Jesus proved himself able to cure some and save the rest.

In order to ensure his essential survival, man has always been able, in a more or less intuitive way, to listen to the call of the superconscious, expressed by a powerful though vague feeling, warning him of the vital errors contained in imaginative exalta-

---

generally considered as normal. Banalization is the ambivalent counterpart of the neurotic convulsion of spiritual desire. It attributes an excessive importance to material and sexual desires, which are considered as the sole meaning of life.

†In French, *angoisse* (German: *Angst*). A more satisfying term would be "anguish" but the term "anxiety" has been used in all Anglo-Saxon psychoanalytical writings.

tions, and inviting him to return to his harmony. This is a fundamental expression—even if it remains often a secret one—of the struggle for satisfying survival. This is the deep feeling that the man Jesus tries to arouse in the people with a strong vital impulse whom he calls.

Biogenetical ethics, derived from the understanding of the psychic evolution linking animals to men,[6] rules out both moralism and amoralism. It enables us to understand that what all the myths call *good* is not, in spite of appearances created by the façade of the narrative, imposed by a deity existing outside of man but by what is divine in man, the superconscious demand for satisfaction, which is the evolutionary fruit of animal instinctivity.

The struggle of all organisms in their search of satisfaction conditioned and is conditioning evolution toward more and more lucidity. The stage of perceptive lucidity is acquired at the animal level: organs of perception and locomotion and perceptive development of space go together; at the human level, the evolutionary stage is that of cognitive lucidity through which man, having become conscious, perceives himself as living in a three-dimensional time. These stages are marked by a more and more manifest expression of the organizing spirit that is immanent to nature and has become, at the human levels the explanation of the world and the valuation of the desires. The most evolved manifestations of the human mind are spiritualization and sublimation whose goal is the organization of the inner world. The fruits of this evolutionary work are truth and goodness. Or to put it in mythical language: creative harmony, manifest in its effects, is the mysterious "Essence." Its evolution through the species eventually reveals the essential desire that is able to oppose the meaningless multiplication of accidental desires and therefore able to accept its function as organizer of the intrapsychic world, the world of desires.

In such a perspective, one can understand that the ethos that is immanent to life is to be capable, if need be, of sacrificing the life of the body to that of the essence; in other words to prefer the death of the body to the death of the soul, a task that the man Jesus fulfilled in all its magnitude.

Seeking lucidity about oneself and one's motivations becomes the ideal of human life. It is the truth about *anthropos* and his quest for satisfaction. The truth about psychic functioning and its laws, about desire and its transformations—the basis of life itself—conditions objective knowledge of the world since the world is the place where the desires can be satisfied. The world is seen quite differently by men, depending on their capacity or incapacity to sublimate the greed of their desires. Thus defined, truth does not appear as absolute but as lawful. The lawful aspect of the truth gives it the possibility of evolving, not in its foundation but in its formulation. Truth and its biogenetical support—harmony—can be defined in various ways. The mythical and symbolic formulation can become conceptual and scientific. Just like images, concepts wear out in time. They have to be renewed. Truth about the psychic functioning evolves since the psyche evolves. But—and this is a fundamental criterion of science—the different formulations of the truth remain analogically linked since no formulation can contradict the others without becoming an error; in this respect, truth is immutable for, we repeat it, it is harmony: "The truth shall make you free," Jesus told the Pharisees (Jn 8:32).

Man, any man, but even more so man when he has a strong vital impulse, is faced with the unfathomable mystery of existence; the outer world and inner life are governed by law: how can this be? To the extent that he becomes aware of this lawful organization, man is frightened and moved. Only the power of superconscious emotion can enable man to perceive, in all its lawfulness, the strength of the preconscious spirit, organizer of all of nature even in its minutest forms.

Trusting the organizing force manifested in all the modalities of the visible world, man symbolizes with the divinity image the modal aspect of this organizing power (which can be found in all things from the atom to the human psyche) and its mysterious and forever unknowable aspect.

In addition to this sense of the mystery of organization, the divinity symbolizes the superconscious process that enables man to organize himself essentially; i.e., to harmonize himself. The divinity, whether seen as the creator of the universe or as the internalized creator of the psyche (the superconscious judge) is a mythical symbol that is at once metaphysical and ethical.

In the Greek myth, Uranus is the creating god and Zeus the law-giving god (law of the superconscious). In the Hindu myth, Brahma is the creating aspect while Vishnu is the conservative one and Shiva the evolutionary one. In the Judaic myth, God is both creator and judge. He cannot be seen face to face, he is the unfathomable mystery from which comes the existing world, but he is also one who speaks confidentially to his prophets, who imposes, demands, and punishes.

In the Christian myth, the creating and judging deity has become God the Father: fear remains only in its sublimated form, the feeling of love of the creature toward its creator. "To be in the hands of the Father" is to rest in an awareness of the mystery and to know that nothing of an insurmountable nature can happen to the man who continues to trust in the lawfulness of life. This is what the Son of Man was able to live fully; he showed by his example that the inexhaustible goodness of life, through the immanence of justice, rewards and punishes men according to their strength or weakness. Thus suffering accepted and overcome is the motor of evolution and the true source of essential satisfaction. Emotion in the face of the mystery of existence is the essentially creative quality of character, since only such a reference to the unfathomable dimension of life governed by lawfulness enables us to dissolve the seduction of imaginative exaltation, of vanity, and to undertake the regulation of the desires. This work of spiritualization-sublimation of the desires is an exceptionally powerful force because it is based on lawfulness: the consequence of spiritualization-sublimation is joy, and the consequence of the exaltation of the desires is either guilty torment (punishment of nervousness) or the death of the vital impulse, the death of feelings (punishment of banalization). It would even be better to say spiritualization-sublimation of the desires is joy, exaltation is inner torment or death.

Thus myths (and the awareness of the mystery at the core of their message) become intelligible through the knowledge of the psychic functioning that alone can enable man to understand to what extent vain autosuggestion kills awe in the face of the unfathomable depths of existence.

Already in the pagan myth, the various human qualities are represented by the various deities; in Greek mythology, Zeus is

lucidity (in other words: he expresses the law of the superconscious since the latter is lucidity about our most hidden motivations). Hera is love, Apollo is harmony, Athena symbolizes the
combativeness of the spirit. The God of Jewish and Christian
monotheism symbolizes by himself all the human qualities condensed in the ultimate expression of the superconscious animating impulse.

It is as incarnation of the supreme qualities of lucidity and
love, expressions of superconscious intensity, that Jesus is called
Son of the Father. Every man is son of the Father, but not in the
same sense as was the man Jesus. Every man is also son of the
devil; i.e., under the obsessive sway of his vain intentions.

That mythical thought is a universal fact is proven by the
possibility inherent in the introspective method of revealing the
significance of the symbols used in the myths of all cultures.
Fundamental symbols such as light, bread, fish, water, the lamb,
the foot were universally used. Myth being a pre-science of
psychic functioning, every mythical symbol represents a psychic
function: material or sexual desires, essential desire, sublime or
perverse imagination, lucid or affective thought, feelings or resentments, superconsciously or subconsciously determined volitions.

The purpose of the images borrowed from the outer world is
to express an essential given of inner life. The transposition from
the plane of the reality of the image to the symbolic plane enables
us to find the psychological significance of the symbol. It is therefore necessary to define the characteristic qualities of the image
that is used. Thus bread is the food of the body, and becomes on
the symbolic plane food for the spirit: the truth. A bird symbolizes the soaring spirit. In order to be able to express a dynamic
relationship between the sublime (superconscious function) and
the perverse (subconscious function), myth uses either attributes
turning positive into negative or vice versa or actions exerted on
a negative function and transforming it into a positive one or vice
versa. Thus a bird can, if its attributes spell it out, represent
exalted spirit and its pseudo-soaring—becoming by this very fact
a negative symbol, for instance the birds of the lake of Stym-
phalus in the myth of Herakles.[7] Moreover, it is possible, and
often necessary, to translate one single symbol with synonymous

terms that are however directed toward different aspects of the psychic functioning. Thus, if we talk about essential desire, about the superconscious or the evolutionary impulse, one single function is evoked. But thanks to the choice of words, essential desire is presented in connection with accidental desires, the superconscious is shown in its antithetic relationship with the subconscious, and the evolutionary impulse is evoked in its biogenetical function.

A bird can therefore be translated in its positive significance by the word spirit or essential desire or superconscious. The consistency of the translation will, we hope, convince the reader of the efficacity of the methodology and the authenticity of symbolism.

Attention should be drawn to the link that can be established with pagan mythology. Several examples, illustrating the procedure while stressing the link between the various myths, will thus prepare the reader for the understanding of the translation of the Gospel of John. In myths, the function of the elucidating spirit is represented by the light-giving sun. Ahura-Mazda (in Persia), Varuna (India), Amon-Ra (Egypt), Zeus (Greece) are all solar deities; finally, Jesus calls himself the light of the world, the spirit of truth that, like the sun, brings light into "the darkness" (symbolizing the subconscious) though the latter "did not understand him."

In all myths, the fish is the symbol of material and sexual drives exalted by vanity and turned into greed, psychologically defined as an expression of banalization; it moves in the deepest depths of the sea (the subconscious); in Greek mythology, Poseidon symbolizes the law ruling the underwater empire, the world of banalization, the law stipulating that man cannot venture into the fallacious promises of exalted material and sexual desires without gradually losing his humanity, without becoming dead in the soul.

In Judaic mythology, Jonah, the prophet called to arouse the inhabitants of Nineveh from the death of the soul, is terrified by the task; in his anxiety when he has to face the world, he forgets the call of his vital impulse and is thus himself swallowed by a big fish, the monster of banalization.

In the Christian myth, the fish taken from the depths of the sea becomes a positive symbol; it is banalization overcome, taken away from its natural milieu, exposed to the light, reducing it to what it really is: a false promise of satisfaction; it is the symbol of the sublimation of exalted desires; Jesus gives bread (spiritual truth) and fishes (sublimation of the perversions) to the crowd that has come to listen to him, he reveals to the crowd the truth about the false promises of banalization, and frees it from them. This is one of the reasons* why the fish became the symbol of nascent Christianity.[8]

The foot is the universal symbol of the soul, of the animating impulse whose energy feeds all the psychic functions and their dynamism. Man has evolved to the erect posture, he alone can perceive the mystery of his animation.

In Greek mythology, the name Oedipus means "swollen foot." Vain swelling is indeed what made Oedipus the very image of the exalted and inhibited neurotic—in spirit as well as in his earthly desires; his criminal and incestuous relationships with his father and mother[9] are the symbol of his perverse relationships with his own spirit (father) and his own desires (mother).

In the Christian myth, Jesus washes the feet of his disciples: he purifies their soul. The episode is translated in detail in this book.

In the Greek and Judeo-Christian myths, wheat, flour, and bread symbolize the truth.

In the mysteries of Eleusis, the grain of wheat shown to the initiates symbolizes the essential task to be accomplished: searching for the truth about earthly desires.

In the Judaic myth, when the Hebrews leave Egypt in Exodus, they take along unleavened bread, symbol of the necessary truth in their quest for the Promised Land.

In the Christian myth, Jesus himself becomes the bread of life, the incarnate truth; the example of his life feeds the vital impulse of those who are seeking a solution to the essential problem. This central symbolism will be explained when the passage is translated.

We must stress that a rigorous analogy between the symbolisms of various cultures is only valid when the myths compared

---

*In addition to the fact that the letters of the Greek word for fish, *Ichthus,* form an anagram, *Iesus CHristus Theou Uios Soter,* which means Jesus Christ, Son of God, Savior.—Translator.

are on the same level of culture (which must not be confused with the same level of civilization). This level of culture is the degree of lucidity attained by the collective superconscious that gives birth to the myths. Thus Egyptian mythology remains imbued with animistic elements and uses, to represent certain deities, fantastic beings half-human, half-animal. Greek, Judaic, or Christian mythologies reserve this imaginative combination for monsters and demons (centaurs, satyrs, the serpent in Paradise, Satan). The humanlike deity of the Greek or Judaic myth (Athene who is always ready to support Ulysses, Yahweh talking with Moses) becomes in the Christian myth the deified man: man himself has become the god who guides him, the vital impulse that leads him, not simply for a short while any more, but definitively so: "The Father and I are one," Jesus says.

Fundamental analogies do therefore persist, linking together the various visions of the human superconscious in the face of the essential problems of life. If all those fabulations had not been animated by the same quest, that of truth about the meaning of life, they would not have been able to create a genuine myth, the expression of the very same intuitive knowledge of the psychic functioning and its relationships with the world, which can therefore be translated according to the same method. They would have copied one another superficially, without however giving any possibility of survival to the spirit of truth, the only one capable of creating a myth.

However, every myth retains its specificity and its proper symbolic expression. The mythical eras influenced one another, but each one of them created new images, new stories. There is an evolution in the way the divinity is grasped; the gods of polytheism are represented by figurative images. Judaic monotheism, attaining a more evolved concept of the symbol God, forbids it to be represented by an image; it is not possible for man to see God face to face, since he is the mystery that will never be known. In the Temple dwells only the name of God (Dt 12:11), "with heaven my throne and earth my footstool" (Is 66:1).

Even if one can regret the rich vision of Greek symbolism in which the qualities and shortcomings of the human soul were represented by a multiplicity of deities and monsters, one can only admire the accuracy of the Judaic vision that, in order to express the intensity of its awe in the face of the mystery of life—

the impossibility of even coming anywhere near its cause—forbids itself to make an anthropomorphic representation of it.

When the god of the Old Testament becomes the god of love of the New Testament, a new evolutionary step has been taken.

But this god of love is at the same time the expression of the lawfulness of life. Just as the avenging god of the Old Testament abandons his people to the hands of its enemies, as a punishment for having forgotten the Covenant with the Almighty (the eternal truth), so the god of love compels each one of us to face the responsibility for his fault (which is the genuine mark of love): "Every hair on your head has been counted" (Mt 10:30).

When Jesus was born, the ancient world was totally decadent: Dionysos, symbol of the unscrupulous unleashing of all the desires—a phenomenon characterizing all decadent eras—was already known all over the world (the ancient world). Now all myths are the creation of a young people. The Jewish people, totally decadent, was therefore not capable any more of producing a myth; Jesus, using ancient mythical images (Son of God) gives new life to the myth.

Though one should not forget the fact that the words related in the Gospels are not the exact words of Jesus, it can be affirmed without the slightest doubt that they are a faithful interpretation of his thought; he himself had undoubtedly known and studied the symbolic language in his youth.

The language of those days used imagery peculiar to the ancient East; it certainly influenced Jesus as well as John. Hellenistic Judaism and Palestinian Judaism were both at home in symbolic thought. Pagan symbolism echoed in the Jewish soul that had been sensitized by scriptural symbolism; the themes of life and rebirth, the images of water and light, the symbolism of filiation are constantly evoked in the Bible. The "Son of God" image was especially common in the Old Testament (see Wis 2:13–20; Jb 1–6; Ps 2:7; Hos 2:1, and so on); the Synoptic Gospels used it and so did John. Did Jesus himself belong to the sect of the Essenes, and did he know esoteric Judaism (the Qumran manuscripts)? Whatever the case may be, he was nurtured by Semitic thought and influenced by Hellenistic syncretism. However, only an exceptionally vigorous vital impulse was able to free itself from the grip of the doctrinal thought of those days and become capable of expressing the universal mythical thought, the eternal truth. And that myth was not only thought but lived.

And even if it had only been superconsciously dreamt, the myth would still be testimony to a hope for a cultural renewal that was indispensable for the Greco-Roman era on its way to total decadence.

The Christian myth spoken by Jesus can be summed up as follows: "I am the Son of God, I came down from Heaven to bring the message of salvation to mankind." This must be understood as follows: Jesus, Son of Man—i.e., man and symbolically Son of God—animated by a quite exceptional and even unique vital impulse, gives up the state of bliss (the Heaven of joy) in which he is, in order to call mankind, given to the slothful ways that typify decadent eras, to emerge from its conventional platitudes and be reborn to spiritual life.

For this purpose he brings to people his message of joy, which was already found in the myth of Perseus and implicitly contained in all of mythology, a simple and clear message: man can overcome the perverse tendency of human nature, the propensity to exaltation of the imagination that is called original sin in the Judaic myth. Thus, in spite of the decadence into which a whole people has fallen, man can individually be reborn, be resurrected from the death of the soul, since imaginative exaltation can be vanquished. As a myth that is experienced, Jesus gives himself the title of "Son of Man." If he were not the Son of Man, his image would not have the same scope. It is because he was himself humanly tempted and was able to overcome the demonic temptations of imaginative exaltation, that his message is of vital importance for the world.[10]

In order to get rid of the guilt awakened in them by this message, men killed the victorious hero. Then, still so as not to have to face the truth that had been offered to them, they turned him into a real god. Could there not also be a new attempt to free themselves from the call, in the denial of the man Jesus' very existence?

All our present moribund values are grounded in the Christian myth. The true significance of this myth was understood only briefly. As early as the first councils, its deep truth was dogmatized and thus lost. The apostle Paul already encountered misunderstandings; he tried to oppose literal interpretation: "The letter kills," he said, "the Spirit is life."

It is understandable that the Church was compelled, in the presence of the many gospels and various Gnostic sects that flourished at that time, to impose articles of faith. But in the process the real scope of the message was lost.

The Synoptic Gospels of Luke and Matthew describe at the beginning of the narrative the temptations of Jesus; i.e., his inner clash with imaginative exaltation, symbolized by Satan.[11] Jesus, overcoming Satan, is recognized as being the Son of God and "angels appeared [symbols of the sublime forces] and looked after him" (Mt 4:11). Throughout all four Gospels, there are signs that Jesus is struggling against inner evil. He himself confesses his anguish and overcomes it with as much humility as force of acceptance:

> Now my soul is troubled. What shall I say:
> Father save me from this hour?
> But it was for this very reason that I have come to this hour.
> Father, glorify your name!
>
> (Jn 12:27–18).

In Mt 27:46; and Mk 15:34, anguish overwhelms him on the cross, "Father, why have you abandoned me?"—an expression of his moving humanity. However, these are only sporadic manifestations. Jesus says (Jn 12:31), "Now the prince of the world is to be overthrown," and this shortly after the washing of the apostles' feet. Accused of being in cahoots with the devil and therefore able to foresee his coming death, Jesus undoubtedly does not evoke in this verse an external triumph but quite certainly a decisive inner victory. This is clearly stated at the end of his teaching, shortly before his arrest (Jn 16:33): "Be brave, I have conquered the world." And faced with the most glaring injustice—given the ignominy of the punishment and the magnitude of the work he accomplished—Jesus exclaims, "Father, forgive them; they do not know what they are doing" (Lk 23:34). This is the purest manifestation of the superconscious, definitive victory. Only at this ultimate moment are any accusation and complaint, and therefore any vain exaltation of the self, eliminated.

Let us reiterate that these words may not have been actually spoken by Jesus. Would people have heard them if they had been whispered at the top of the cross? They do, however, express the exceptional capacity of sublimation that was rightly credited to the Son of Man; they are the fruit of the superconscious; they are, at the least, the tangible proof of human thought's dimension.

The torture of crucifixion in itself, seen from the viewpoint of the legal practices of that time, has recently been questioned. It may be that Jesus did not die on the cross but simply on the gallows, or in another way.

The cross, which has a profoundly symbolic significance, may have been used later on to round out the myth. The symbol of the cross stands for the coordinates—horizontal and vertical—of life, on which man is impaled. The whole meaning of life is to achieve harmoniously the complementarity of the vertical dimension—the vital impulse—and the horizontal one—earthly desires.

In the framework of the myth, Jesus is the Son of Man, he died achieving the deep significance of human life: the reconciliation of the vital impulse with the accidental conditions of life, in this case the hatred of the world that he fully accepted and overcame. Thus the Christian myth, like all myths, is based on the struggle of the hero against his own weakness, a necessary condition to acquire the right to offer truth to the world. However, it will be very enlightening to point out briefly the differences between the Christian myth and the myth of Perseus, the victorious hero of Greek symbolism.

The central episode of the myth of Perseus is his struggle with Medusa, the difficulty of victory over his vanity, and the conditions for such a victory not to become vanity over his victory. All sorts of adventures (the encounter with the three Graces, the search for the nymphs, etc.) tell how Perseus prepares himself for the struggle. Everything leads to the struggle, symbol of the combat against the inner evil.

However, Perseus, like Jesus, is confronted by the perverse forces that support the world, symbolized by the Titan Atlas, who, wishing to turn his back on the message of joy, refuses hospitality to the hero who had overcome vanity.[12] But this significant episode remains of secondary importance in the framework of the myth.

On the other hand, the four Gospels, even though they tell of the inner struggle of Jesus, stress above all the sublime struggle of the hero against the evil of the world, the conventionality of the spirit and the unquenchable greed of the desires or banalization. His public life is a tireless call to men whose vital impulses, though disoriented, are enduring.

In the Christian myth, the story starts with Jesus' victory over Satan. Thus Jesus talks only about the mystery of existence in which every man is called to rest, and about the manifest expression of this unfathomable mystery: the lawfulness of the visible world.

In order to overcome Satan—exalted love of the self—one must effectively understand that the Heaven of joy, the ultimate reward given by life, can be attained only by those who free themselves from the greed of accidental desires and thereby discover the other side of life, namely its sublime dimension.

The opposite discovery is that exalted attachment to earthly desires can only bring guilty torture or inner death.

What is stressed in the Gospels, and especially in the Gospel of John, is the permanence of one essential theme, which appears again and again in the various episodes of the narration and the symbolic formulations whose purposeful repetition is a methodical means of imbuing people's minds with the truth. The apostle Paul himself tirelessly repeated the same themes throughout his epistles.

Just as, in Judeo-Christian symbolic thought, all the human qualities are concentrated in the one symbol of God, so the sole cause of disorientation, oblivion of the essential, becomes in the Johannine Gospel, the central point from which everything else proceeds. The diversity of psychic constellations, stressed in the Greek myth, is not the goal of the Christian myth. The Gospels show that misunderstanding of essential life is the only cause of all the psychic maladies and all the miseries of life. Which is why the same teaching is given by Jesus, whether it be to the paralytic (neurotic), the man blind from birth (banal), or the dead in the soul (banalized). The Old Testament was already centered around the Covenant (with God), symbol of the love for the essential; all the ills of the Jewish people come from its oblivion of the Covenant.

The repetitive method used all through the Gospels is meant to convince the disciples little by little, to prepare them to accept in their turn the meaning of life, to receive the "Holy Spirit," symbolized by the Paraclete; i.e., to become capable of understanding the dimension of life, its evolutionary direction, the task that the valuating spirit must undertake in order to become incarnate, to animate man even in his bodily expressions and daily activities.

> Jn 15:15 "I call you friends
> Because I have made known to you
> Everything I have learned from
> my Father [Superconscious],"

Jesus tells them, shortly before his death. The insistence with which Jesus repeats his essential proposition: essential life is more important than accidental life—learn to see the mysterious organization standing behind all that you can see since this is our only certainty—this insistence becomes the story of an actual experience.

For many people, this proof of the reality of Jesus, being above all a psychological one, will not be convincing. They will be more easily convinced by the verse 14 of John's Prologue: "The Word was made flesh,/He lived among us [he pitched his tent among us]/And we saw his glory . . ." and so on. In the detailed translation of this verse, we will show that the evolutionary Spirit (the Word) can be fully embodied in man. When we look at the full magnitude of the problem, it is not really that important whether Jesus actually lived or not. The myth of the incarnation and its evolutionary and cosmic scope endure through time. The incarnation of spirit in matter will be made more and more manifest (see the translation of the Prologue). The proposition of the Christian myth is a decisive evolutionary step with respect to the Judaic myth: man can detach himself from the culture in which he was born so as to undertake by himself his essential survival (culture being the totality of the valuations wrought by past generations, valuations that underlie the deliberation of the individual but wind up being sclerotic and lead to the decadence of the culture).

What the myth shows is the dimension, the tremendous scope of life, when the struggle against "demons and monsters" is largely won, when the fight against and the dissolution of vanity and the rancors it begets have become a daily practice: then joy and peace become possible, always relative, but as a consequence of an inner certainty about the essential of life; this is why Jesus tells his disciples (14:27), "My own peace I give you" and again,

> (16:22), ". . . your hearts will be full of joy,/
> And that joy, no one shall take from you."

He is talking to fallible men and he is aware of it, yet he calls them, when he feels that they are mature enough to understand, to find the peaceful joy of certainty. Not only is joy possible, but also love (20:12–13). One does not go without the other, the dissolution of exalted desires is love of one's essential self and love of the essential self of the other, thus sublime joy. All that is not rooted in this task of spiritualization-sublimation is vain exaltation and accidental agitation.

Such is the message of the Gospel. The essential task is the glory of the human spirit, and its glorification. This is why, when Jesus enters Jerusalem, a voice from Heaven exclaims (12:28), "I have glorified it and I will glorify it again." This voice symbolizes the temporary enthusiasm of those who are capable of understanding what is happening; even the crowd heard (12:29), which means that it is not insensitive to the greatness of Jesus' stance.

The Christian myth was not created by a people, but a reborn people, the real Christian people, that of the first century after the death of Jesus, made up of all those—Jews, Greeks, people of the Hellenized lands—whose vital impulse was aroused by the example of the Galilean, this new people takes the myth that Jesus had proposed and perfects it. It adds the miraculous birth of the "Child God" born of a virgin and the Holy Spirit (Matthew and Luke) an element that is in conformity with all mythologies: the superconscious in all its power (the mythical Father) is the true creator of the victorious hero; in Greek mythology, Zeus, in the guise of a shower of gold, impregnates the virgin Danae, mother of Perseus; as to the image of the virgin mother, symbol of the purity of earthly desires, the psychic heritage of the victorious hero, it is found in all myths.

The mythical vision, springing from the superconscious, invents the episode of the Magis: the powers of the world come from all over, guided by the star that symbolizes the ideal, in order to worship the hope that the newborn infant means for all mankind. This legendary aspect whose origin is mythical is based on a wish to establish a link between the Old and the New Testament and to show that the Messiah had always been expected and foreseen. He was expected, and he came in the form of the man Jesus. But what had been predicted was the coming of the victorious hero who was to come in any event, since mankind periodically begets its prophets, founders of a new culture. The visionary force of the myth enables it to predict the essential future of the human species, without any accidental element. It was not Jesus who had been announced but Christ, the Lord's anointed, the truth incarnate. The apostle Paul greatly contributed to this mythical development. He uses the words *death* and *resurrection*, which were already common in the Old Testament in their symbolic meaning of death of the soul and resurrection during life. He turns this into Christian language *par excellence*: he adds to the word *death* a new significance, "death to sin," synonymous with resurrection.

Once dogmatized, the symbolic vocabulary and the miraculous episodes of the legend lose their mythical meaning; death becomes real death, and resurrection, the resurrection of the body after death, at the last judgment.

Understanding the evangelical message is a step forward in the search for truth; it is part of the spirit's striving for more lucidity. The spirit must become capable of analyzing its own productions, from the most sublime to the most perverse, myths, dreams, and psychopathological symptoms. Any evolutionary process is a process of intensification of life, a possibility of a richer harmony.

To understand symbolic thought would be the only solution for so many minds who go astray, either in the belief in images or in the mockery of these images. A reconciliation between the materialists who deny any significance to the mythical symbol of divinity, and the spiritualists who consider it as a reality, can only take place in the understanding of symbolism. This implies knowledge that mythical symbols represent psychic functions and that mythical stories are an extremely precise description, full of nuances, of the psyche's functioning. Only a methodical research would free from their antiscientific lack of precision those who presently hold psychological theories devoid of any biogenetic foundation. Man, in our scientific era, is, when it comes to his inner life, greatly under the sway of beliefs, or to put it in other words: of superstitions, be they spiritualistic or materialistic. Having lost the superconscious understanding of mythical symbolism, he runs the risk of regressing to a simplistic vision of the world, eliminating the mysterious dimension of life and its immanent biological meaning. The attempt to understand the meaning of life is bound to fail so long as people do not grasp the full scope and importance of symbolic thought even in daily life where daydreams and psychopathological symptoms are manifested in their specific language.

Through conceptual explanation, the genuine understanding of symbolic images leads back to the emotion that brought forth these symbols whose beauty is so surprising and that contain such a deep understanding of life and its meaning.

To quote the Evangelist (Jn 3:8),

"The wind blows wherever it pleases;
You hear its sound,
But you cannot tell where it comes from or where it is going."

It blows for whoever is mature enough to seek out the truth.

Part 1

THE PROLOGUE OF
THE GOSPEL OF JOHN

CHAPTER 2

The Myth of the Incarnation

Among all the texts of the New Testament, the Prologue of John's Gospel is one of the least anecdotal, one of the most purely symbolic. It condenses and generalizes in a striking way the mythical story of the world and of life and shows the eternally exemplary scope and the evolutionary significance of the phenomenon of sanctification that, in the Judeo-Christian cultural cycle to which we belong, is illustrated by the life and heroic death of the man Jesus.

The Gospels (literally, "the good news") relate the life and words of Jesus. He showed through his life that "original sin" (the exaltation of desires) could be overcome, that the inner conflict could be appeased by a definitive reversal of the calculus of satisfaction, consciously seeking the conservation at all costs of inner harmony, the "life of the soul," be it at the cost of the life of the body. The example becomes a source of hope for all of mankind.

But the Gospels are not only narrative. The Evangelists, and especially John (and also the apostle Paul), grasped the general and even cosmic scope of Jesus' example. They understood that his life was the inimitable but guiding achievement of man's latent possibilities. Thus, with all their emotion, they recognized in Jesus the "Christ," the "Messiah," the one who actually fulfilled the meaning of life, whose symbolic expression was the constant theme of the Old Testament.

Genesis relates how pathological suffering appeared with conscious being: the Old Testament in its entirety describes the effort, often impotent, of mankind (symbolized by the Chosen People) to live in essential satisfaction (symbolically, the Covenant) and to escape pathological suffering (symbolically, punishment by Yahweh). The New Testament shows that there is, for the individual, a possibility to find the way to joy, even in the midst of a completely decadent world. The Prologue of John's Gospel shows that this possibility is in conformity with the evolutionary meaning of life, enlightening its past and foreshadowing its future.

This terse digest of the meaning of the Prologue indicates from the outset that symbolic exegesis is radically different from literal and dogmatic exegesis. The text of the Prologue of John, taken literally, is the source of the dogma of the Incarnation, a fundamental dogma of official Christianity that claims to explain God's intentions and nature rationally. Now, this text is fundamental when it comes to understanding the *symbolic* meaning of the Christian myth. According to literal exegesis, Jesus is not a man, he is the Word, a real God preexistent from the beginning and deciding at a given moment to take a human form. For symbolic exegesis, the Prologue of John is the source of the *myth* and not of the *dogma* of the incarnation. The myth of the incarnation is the symbolically profound explanation of life in evolution. It was created by the superconscious and veracious imagination to soothe metaphysical anguish with the certitude that suffering can be overcome and that the mysterious evolutionary intentionality immanent in life (symbolically: "God's purpose," the "Word of God") is in itself benevolent and intelligible in its manifestations. In symbolic exegesis *God the Father symbolizes the unfathomable mystery of the Origins, the Word symbolizes the manifest appearance, and the Son symbolizes the evolutionary hope of mankind*, meanings that will be explained further on. Thus the Prologue of John is not only the source of the myth of the incarnation, but also of the myth of the trinity.[13] The Trinity is the symbolically profound expression of man's religious feeling awakened by the mystery of the Origins and the mystery of life in evolution. Dogmatism, confusing in a single actual person the two symbolic persons— the Word (second person) and the Son (third person)—makes any understanding impossible. Dogma thus believes itself compelled to add a third person—the Holy Spirit, who does not appear at all in the Prologue of John. On the other hand, the symbolic trinity: Father, Word, and Son is the central theme of the Prologue. It is the only genuine trinity, and its significance is the same as that of the myth of the incarnation, which it sums up and generalizes. Here is the traditional text of John's Prologue:

1 In the beginning was the Word:
  the Word was with God
  and the Word was God.
2 He was with God in the beginning.
3 Through him all things came to be,
  Not one thing had its being but through him.
4 All that came to be had life in him
  and that life was the light of men,
5 a light that shines in the dark,
  a light that darkness could not overpower.

6 A man came, sent by God.
  His name was John.
7 He came as a witness,
  as a witness to speak for the light,
  so that everyone might believe through him.
8 He was not the light,
  only a witness to speak for the light.

9 The Word was the true light
  that enlightens all men;
  and he was coming into the world.
10 He was in the world
  that had its being through him,
  and the world did not know him.
11 He came to his own domain
  and his own people did not accept him.
12 But to all who did accept him
  He gave power to become children of God,
  to all who believe in the name of him
13 who was born not of human stock
  or urge of flesh
  or will of man
  but of God himself.
14 The Word was made flesh,
  he lived among us,
  and we saw his glory,
  the glory that is his as the only Son of the Father,
  full of grace and truth.

15 John appears as a witness. He proclaims:
"This is the one of whom I said:
He who comes after me
ranks before me
because he existed before me."

16 Indeed, from his fullness we have, all of us, received
yes, grace in return for grace,
17 since, though the Law was given through Moses
grace and truth have come through Jesus Christ.
18 No one has ever seen God;
it is the only Son, who is nearest to the Father's heart,
who has made him known.

The purpose of this study is not to engage in an argument with dogma. However, dogmatic belief (which is a historical necessity but an involutionary stagnation in the essential history of human thought) is so deeply attached to the superstitious interpretation of the incarnation that it is necessary to confront dogmatic interpretation more rigorously with symbolic exegesis so as to uncover the deep meaning of the myth of the incarnation.

The crucial point is this: as far as dogma is concerned, the Word is a truly preexistent deity, entirely identified with Jesus. As far as symbolic exegesis goes, the Word is a symbol, while Jesus is a real man. The central affirmation of the Prologue: "the Word was made flesh" is for dogma the account of an actual event, while for symbolic exegesis it is a symbolic expression endeavoring to show the real scope of the man Jesus' achievement. Starting from a false premise—namely that the biblical texts have to be understood literally—dogmatic exegesis is compelled, through a *logical* deduction based on an *erroneous* first assumption, to launch a whole series of affirmations, the absurdity of which becomes so patent that the theologians themselves, since they cannot deny it, pretend to use it as a proof: "I believe *because* it is absurd. *"Credo quia absurdum."* In the Prologue of John, misunderstanding of the symbolism in "the Word was made flesh" leads to a total identification of the Word with Jesus. The result is, among others, an interpretation of verse 3, according to which all things "came to be" through Jesus since all things "came to be" through the Word.

For dogma, it is all the more difficult to get rid of such an interpretation since verse 10 takes it up again: "the world that had its being through him." *Jesus is the creator of the world.* The logical conclusion of such a conception is expressed in the final (eighteenth) verse, which sums up the dogmatic significance of Christian theology:

> No one has ever seen God;
> it is the only Son, who is nearest to the Father's heart,
> who has made him known.

Thus, according to dogma, before Jesus (who was erroneously thought of as being only a man by his contemporaries, with the exception of a few chosen ones) appeared in Galilee, the world (undoubtedly one must understand by this the cosmos with its billions of galaxies) *knew nothing about the real nature of God. And since then it does!* The Catholic Church is seen as the depository of this revelation and transmits it to whoever wishes to incorporate himself into the Church through the rites of baptism and communion.

If the texts can lend themselves to a coherent reading eliminating absurdity, the least one can say is that such a reading deserves to be taken into consideration.

CHAPTER 3

Textual Problems

Before going into the details of symbolic exegesis, certain points concerning the structure of the text must be studied in the light of the preceding observations.

A critical reading of the Prologue and of the first chapter of John's Gospel cannot fail to uncover the heterogeneous nature of the Prologue. It is quite clear that two elements exist side by side and that they are clumsily combined: on the one hand, the symbolic narrative dealing with God, the Word, the Word made flesh, the Only Son, and Jesus Christ; on the other hand, an anecdotal narrative in verses 6, 7, 8, 9, and 15, containing the historical testimony of John the Baptist. The account of this testimony, the annunciation of the preaching of Jesus takes up, in fact, most of the first chapter, after the Prologue (verses 19 to 38).

Since the very purpose of dogmatism is precisely to make of the historical Jesus a supernatural person by identifying him with the Word taken for a reality, one can understand that zealous priests wished to put into the Prologue an element of miraculous prediction, making of John the Baptist—the historical forerunner of Jesus—the annunciator of the miracle. The theologians thus found it opportune to use the testimony of John the Baptist to strengthen the belief in a real Incarnation of the Word, itself a reality.

Mixing in this manner history and symbolism, this interpolation (for that is what it is!) manages to induce a belief—in those who are willing—that the Incarnation is a supernatural event, miraculously announced by a prophet who was actually inspired by God himself. Symbolism and history, thus confused, acquire one from the other the appearance of a supernatural and miraculous meaning.

In verse 6, the appearance of John the Baptist—"A man came, sent by God . . ."—abruptly interrupts the general theme without any transition and without any justification (except the dogmatic ones). The purpose of this interpolation is to have John the Baptist announce the "miracle" of the Incarnation: "The Word was made flesh . . ."

Not only does verse 6 break the continuity, but the latter is reestablished if one removes the sequence of verses 6 to 9 from the Prologue.

Verses 4 and 5 are thus quite naturally continued in verse 10:

> 4 All that came to be had life in *him*
> and that life was the light of men
> 5 a light that shines in the dark,
> a light that darkness could not overpower.
> 10 *He* was in the world
> that had its being through him,
> and the world did not know him.

It is quite clear that verses 4 and 10 deal with the Word and not with Jesus: Jesus is not the creator of the world, but the world is, symbolically speaking, the manifestation of the Word.

The same kind of remark is valid for verse 15, the purpose of which is to confirm that Jesus is indeed he whose supernatural coming has been announced by John the Baptist. As in the case of the previous interpolation, this verse 15 breaks the continuity, which is clearly reestablished once we remove the interpolation. Indeed, verse 14 talks about "us" (all those who have understood the message of Jesus) and continues quite naturally in verse 16:

> 14 The Word was made flesh,
> he lived among *us*,
> and *we* saw his glory,
> the glory that is his as the only Son of the Father,
> *full of grace* and truth.
> 16 Indeed from his fullness, we have, all of us, received
> yes, grace in return for grace.

Thus the Prologue recovers its symbolic purity and all its cosmic and metaphysical grandeur embracing the past and future of evolution.

On the other hand, by putting back the verses we have removed from the Prologue to their natural place—i.e., after verse 18, and at the beginning of the evangelical narrative itself—we can see that the historical testimony of John the Baptist is now reconstituted in its integrity.

This testimony continues after verse 15 with the more anecdotal account of John the Baptist's relationship with the traditional ecclesiastical authorities (verse 19 and following).

Without any doubt, this simple solution is a shock for those who have a conventional and literal respect for the texts as they stand; our hypothesis is based on the method of symbolic deciphering, and a detailed study of the Prologue will simply confirm it.

Here is the transcription of the text of the Prologue (as we have reconstituted it), followed by the beginning of the evangelical text:

> In the beginning was the Word:
> The Word was with God
> and the Word was God.
> He was with God at the beginning.
> Through him all things came to be,
> Not one thing had its being but through him.
> All that came to be had life in him
> and that life was the light of men,
> a light that shines in the dark,
> a light that darkness could not overpower.
>
> He was in the world
> that had its being through him,
> and the world did not know him.
> He came to his own domain
> and his own people did not accept him.
> But to all who did accept him
> he gave power to become children of God,
> to all who believe in the name of him
> who was born not out of human stock
> or urge of flesh
> or will of man
> but of God himself.

The Word was made flesh,
he lived among us,
and we saw his glory,
the glory that was his as the only Son of the Father,
full of grace and truth.

Indeed, from his fullness we have all of us, received
yes, grace in return for grace,
since, though the Law was given through Moses
grace and truth have come through Jesus Christ.
No one has ever seen God;
it is the only Son, who is nearest to the Father's heart
who has made him known.

A man came, sent by God,
His name was John.
He came as a witness,
as a witness to speak for the light,
so that everyone might believe through him.
He was not the light,
only a witness to speak for the light.

The Word was the true light
that enlightens all men;
and he was coming into the world.

John appears as a witness. He proclaims:
"This is the one of whom I said:
He who comes after me
ranks before me
because he existed before me."

This is how John appeared as a witness, When the Jews sent priests and Levites from Jerusalem to ask him, [etc.]

The Prologue thus comprises 13 verses[14] and can be divided into three parts.

The first part (verses 1, 2, and 3) is metaphysical. It deals with the mystery symbolically called God and its relationship with the Word, which symbolizes the appearance (of the manifest world).

The second part (verses 4, 5, 10, 11, 12, 13) deals with the relationship between the Word and man, who is more or less capable of being moved by the awareness of mystery deeply enough for this to motivate his activity. In this sense, the second part sums up the profound meaning of the Old Testament, which is precisely the responsibility of the human being in relation to the meaning of life, which is both mysterious and manifest.

The third part (verses 14, 16, 17, 18) of the Prologue *and only this part* refers to the man Jesus, symbolically called Son of God or Incarnate Word, for he is rightly considered by the Christian myth as the example of the achievement toward which is directed not only mankind since its origins symbolized by the birth of Adam, but also all life in evolution symbolized by the Word of God. This is why he is also called the Only Son since he foreshadows the only hope of mankind to overcome by evolution the suffering of Adam's sin.

The Prologue of John therefore has a metaphysical and an ethical significance. In its ethical aspect, it presents Jesus as a victorious hero, he who has overcome the sin of Adam. The metaphysical meaning is still more essential: the sanctified man is shown as the clearest, most condensed, most evolved manifestation of the intentionality immanent in nature, an intentionality that is just as mysterious in its origin as it is manifest in the existence of the organized world, and that the myth calls "Word of God." In its deepest meaning, the Prologue of John does not deal mainly with the man Jesus, a historical reality, but with Christ, a symbol, and with the Only Son, also a symbol. Christ is the eternal truth entirely incarnate in the achievement of Jesus. The Only Son is the evolutionary hope actualized by this accomplishment, and that concerns all mankind.

CHAPTER 4

Deciphering the Verses

VERSES 1 AND 2

> In the beginning was the Word:
> the Word was with God
> and the Word was God.
> He was with God in the beginning.

The initial verses express in a symbolic and extremely condensed form the epistemological foundation of human thought, the fundamental certitude at which thought necessarily arrives when it pursues right to the end its questioning about existence and its origin.

It is quite significant that the mythical explanation posits as a primary evidence "the Word" and as a secondary evidence indissolubly linked to the first, "God." What is the meaning of this "Word"?

"Verbum" is simply the Latin translation of the Greek *logos*, which means literally speech, coherent language, word. The Logos is the Word, the word of God.

1. It is the manifestation of God's will. It thus symbolizes the fact, evident to the spirit though inaccessible to the intellect, that the existing world can neither be conceived as an effect without a cause (*ex nihilo* creation) nor as the effect of a knowable cause (real God or absolute matter). It can be conceived by man only as the effect of an unknowable cause necessarily imagined as proportionate to the vastness of the effect: this cause can only be imagined in an anthropomorphic manner as if all existing phenomena were the expression of the will of a superhuman being.

The Logos is thus the emergence into appearance of the mystery called God, both the intention and the expression of the mysterious cause: both the creative act and the created world.

2. The existence of the world cannot be separated from its organization. The Logos is thus lawfulness, the basic coherence of the world, the foundation of trust in life (mythical faith), and of the explainability of phenomena (scientific faith). It expresses the fundamental evidence that the world is organized according to laws.

In Greek philosophy, this term is constantly used to denote the intentionality immanent in nature, the intelligible organization, which is manifest in its effects but mysterious as to its origins, and which underlies all existing phenomena. The word *logos* is, moreover, akin to "law," "legality," "logic."

3. Lastly, the image of speech, of a discourse taking place in time is very suited to symbolize the temporal unfolding of evolution, mythically conceived as the progressive explicitation of divine intentionality. It is the world in evolution bearing in itself its own law, its own dynamics, its own mysterious animating impulse through which life creates forms of harmony that are more and more complex and intense.

The Prologue states that "in the beginning"—i.e., as far as the human spirit can go back in time—it perceives the Word or Logos, spatiotemporal existence and its organization, without which nothing is given, nothing is conceivable. But it adds immediately that the Word, the Logos, is "with God." If one understands symbolism, this way of thinking is coherent. Indeed, for the spirit, the first evidence is the existence of an organized world; but there is a second evidence that is just as fundamental (and that is totally forgotten by materialistic rationalism): *the mysterious aspect of appearance*, the fact that the perceptible and explainable world is necessarily conceived by man as the effect of a cause remaining forever unperceivable and unexplainable for the human mind. The evangelist immediately adds this second evidence, the awareness of the mysterious foundation of existence, to the first evidence of the existence of an organized world. For these two epistemologically profound evidences are connected by the fact that mystery has a twofold aspect: *the mysterious aspect of manifest organization* (the Word of God) and the *unknowable "cause"* (God the Creator). The mystery of organization is linked to the mystery of the Origins. The last verse of the Prologue will in fact conclude with a new affirmation of the mystery of the Origins: "no one has ever seen God" (verse 18).

After having affirmed at the outset the fundamental duality, appearance (Logos) and mystery (God), and having noted that only appearance, the organized world, actually exists (at the beginning) but that it cannot be conceived outside of the mystery of the Origins (the Word is with God), the evangelist synthesizes again this duality with the phrase "and the Word was God."

These two concepts of mystery and appearance must be separated, but this separation is extremely dangerous: the mystery can be turned into an entity, a mysterious thing or being. The phrase "the Word was God" means that, in fact, for human thought, only one given exists, which is neither mystery nor appearance (mythically speaking neither God nor Word) but existence under its twofold aspect: its manifestly but mysteriously organized aspect (the Word) and its forever incomprehensible aspect: the mystery of its origins (God).

Appearance thus has a mysterious aspect and the mystery is not *mystery in itself* but the *mystery of appearance*. This synthetic complementarity, which is a necessary correction to the analytical duality, is expressed in the formula "and the Word was God."

The very same epistemological truth is expressed in the Prologue of John, the Hebrew Genesis, the Greek Theogony, and in fact in all mythologies.

Primitive man does not perceive the world as an organized entity, but as a succession of phenomena subject to strange and frightening changes. In the mythical era, fear of the environment is already sublimated: the world is superconsciously experienced as being the creation of a benevolent intentionality.

Through the evolutionary process of progressive spiritualization, the emotionally compact notion of mystery becomes diversified and enriched by the growing evidence of *the mystery of the organization* of the cosmos (the Greek word *cosmos*, like the Latin *mundus* and the French *monde*, means "order"). First the contemplation, and then the methodical study of its mysterious lawfulness become more and more direct sources of emotion, provided that man acknowledges the unfathomable mystery of the Origins and gives up any attempt to explain it.

VERSE 3

> Through him all things came to be[15]
> Not one thing had its being but through him.

This verse sums up the purely metaphysical part of the Prologue. "Through him all things came to be" means that there is no existing or possible phenomenon, whatever its nature, whatever the time and place of its occurrence, that does not have an aspect that is forever unexplainable (its very existence), that is not analogically linked to all other phenomena, and that is not included in the evolutionary dynamics of existence.

"Not one thing had its being but through him" is the corollary of the previous statement. This phrase precludes any possibility of metaphysical speculation vainly trying to prove that a supernatural being, thing, or event could exist without being bound by natural laws (spiritualism) or that there can be a being, a thing, or an event whose existence could be entirely conceivable and explainable without any reference to mystery.

The latter approach leads necessarily to the dogmatic materialism that is now in fashion and that, denying the mysterious though manifest intentionality, is compelled to bring in the pseudo-explanation of the concept of chance, which is just as unacceptable for the human mind as the pseudoexplanation of the will of an actually existing God.

Thus it is not an exaggeration to say that the first part of the Prologue of John, in its striking brevity and simplicity, formulates the epistemological foundation of human thought, the basis of the certitude on which a coherent vision of the world and life can be built.

VERSE 4

> All that came to be had life in him
> and that life was the light of men.

This verse constitutes a transition between the first two parts of the Prologue. Since the Prologue is the source of the myth of the incarnation, it can also be said that the first part deals with the primary incarnation or creation or in other words, with the appearance of organized matter, or materialized organization. The second part deals with the incarnation of the spirit in mankind in the form of reflective consciousness and ethical conscience. (The third part will deal with the complete incarnation of the enlightening spirit in the *sanctified man*.) Starting with verse 4, the Word, the manifest and mysterious animating impulse, is no longer considered only as the mysterious aspect of the world in evolution. It becomes specifically the vital force that kindles, "lights up" life and finally enlightens the human psyche.

"All that came to be had life in him" refers to the mysterious source of life seen as a biological phenomenon, the dynamics through which the inner world seeks a more and more intense union with the outer world.[16]

But the Prologue, unlike Genesis, does not develop the diversification of the animating impulse into the countless species out of which will finally emerge the human one; here, the evangelist almost immediately deals with the human stage of evolution; i.e., "and that life was the light of men." This fourth verse establishes a link between the three words: *Word, life,* and *light.*

In the Christian myth, the "Logos" or "Word" symbol belongs exclusively to the Prologue of John. On the other hand, "life" and "light" are frequent symbolic expressions in all myths, and in the Judeo-Christian one in particular.

The word *life* throughout the Bible, and in the Gospels and in the Epistles of Paul in particular, is frequently opposed to the word *death*, just as the word *light* is opposed to the word *darkness*, as is the case in verse 5.

It is therefore indispensable to introduce for the word *life*, besides the biological meaning already noted, the psychological significance that is constantly encountered in biblical writings and that alone can explain how *life* can become "the light of men."

In the same way as death appears constantly in Scripture as the symbol of death of the soul, of banalization, so does life constantly appear under its meaning of life of the soul, essential joy, harmonious activation of thoughts and feelings, concord with oneself and the environment and therefore with the meaning of life.

If the Word, is (in this way) considered as source of life, it is because man is essentially alive insofar as he is essentially animated, motivated by the very same vital impulse that is incarnate in the preconscious being under the form of instinct and that becomes on the human level a superconscious and guiding force. "That life was the light of men" because the only criterion man has for truth or essential error about the meaning of life comes from his deeply felt experience of being psychically "alive," of feeling his vital impulse in action.

Man is alone in his quest for essential satisfaction: the harmonization of his desires. No one outside himself dictates to him what he must do with his life in order to attain essential joy. Yet, this very same immanent organizing and harmonizing spirit manifest in the "blind" intentionality of preconscious life, blossoms in the human psyche in the form of an intuitive knowledge—which is more than conscious, superconscious—of the conditions for essential satisfaction, for harmonization. The sureness of the animal's grasping reflex becomes the certitude of man's reflective grasp of life. Mythically expressed, it is the animating Word that becomes, reflected by the conscious psyche, the valuating, enlightening, "light of men."

VERSE 5

> A light that shines in the dark,
> a light that darkness could not overpower.

This verse sums up all the ethical meaning of the Old Testament. Indeed, the deep meaning of the Judaic myth is that the spirit, having organized matter since the beginning, ceases on the human level to be instinctive and constitutive and becomes guiding and superconscious. This is why the call of the spirit can be ignored and repressed. However, it does not cease to be manifested in the form of essential guiltiness symbolized in the Old Testament by the call of Yahweh.

The light shining in the dark is the truth "shouting in the marketplace" as the psalmist says. This eternal truth cannot impose itself, since the "darkness" of the subconscious, of the repressing process, continues to rebel generation after generation against the elucidating influence of the superconscious. The light is the light in man, and the darkness is the darkness in man, as for instance the following passage from the first epistle of John shows:

> 1 Jn 2:8 "Anyone who claims to be in the light
> but hates his brother
> is still in the dark."

There are many passages of Scripture that oppose the light of superconscious elucidation to the darkness of repression that prevents man, blinded by imaginative exaltation, from grasping the truth about himself and life.

Verse 5 is generally seen as a reference to the incomprehension and hostility encountered by Jesus among his contemporaries. Such an interpretation does not agree, as we have seen, either with the translation of symbolism or even with dogmatic exegesis. It is true that for dogma, Jesus is the Word and the Light but it is only in verse 14 that it is written that the Word was made flesh.

Thus, according to the present explanation, there is absolutely no allusion to the preaching of Jesus before verse 14. Verse 5 therefore deals with light in general, with the truth. It remains true that verses 6, 7, and 8 also deal with light. But it is precisely this fact that permitted the interpolation of these verses in the Prologue. The similarity of the theme (light) was used to slip in three verses after verse 5. However, as we shall see, the light in these verses is the truth *brought by Jesus*, symbolically called Christ.

Jesus, in fact, uses the same image when he talks about himself:

> Jn 12:46 "I, the light, have come into the world
> so that whoever believes in me
> need not stay in the dark any more."

Here Jesus talks about truth in general and his preaching in particular. This similarity in images only stresses the depth of analogy linking the Old and New Testaments, the myth of Yahweh, whose call is heard but often rejected (Adam's sin), and the myth of Christ, whose call remains misunderstood by most people.

VERSE 10

> He (the Word) was in the world
> that had its being through him,
> and the world did not know him[18]

This verse is difficult to understand because the term "world" (*cosmos*) is used here successively in its two different meanings, both of which are constantly encountered in the New Testament. The world created by the Word is the universe, harmoniously organized existence in its entirety.

The world "that did not know him" is the banalized world, the society of men who are too blinded by their affect to be moved by the feeling of mystery, by true religious faith. It is in the latter meaning that Jesus talks about his kingdom "which is not of this world," a phrase generally understood by dogmatism as the promise of a better fate in the beyond, whereas the belief in an actual beyond is totally alien to Judaic thought and, in fact, unacceptable for human thought in general if the latter is based on a coherent epistemology.

The verse sums up again the fundamental theme that is found throughout the Old Testament. The intentionality immanent in nature is at the same time manifest and mysterious. It is the lawful and evolutionary organization of the outer and inner world, thus also of the human psyche in which the preconscious intentionality of the animal is dispersed into multiple intentions, which, however, still remain under the law of harmony, as does all that exists. *But man, alone among all beings, can survive physically while being subjected to psychic disharmony.* He can let his feeling of being mysteriously animated, his vital impulse, die in him. Blinded by the massive affect of his desires, he can let die in him the religious feeling, the emotion awakened in him by the mysterious aspect of what he perceives and of what he is. He can ignore the Word, refuse to know it, refuse to know the essence of life, the meaning of life.

VERSE 11

> He came to his own domain
> and his own people did not accept him.

This verse spells out the meaning of the preceding one. All myths symbolize the intentionality of nature by anthropomorphizing it (it cannot be otherwise). The "will" and "wisdom" of God are imagined by analogy with the will and wisdom of man. Conversely, the myth conceives the half-conscious intentionality of man as a particular case of intentionality in general: "God created man in his image."

The same vision is expressed here in the more impersonal form, which is that of the Prologue. "[The Word] came to his own domain" means that the intentionality diffuse in all nature becomes specific, is progressively incarnated, and, at the most advanced evolutionary stage, becomes human intentionality diversified in multiple intentions. The preconsciously organizing spirit becomes consciously valuating and explanatory.

But the conscious (or rather, still half-conscious) psyche of man is not only spirit,[19] it is also intellect. The spirit looks for a meaningful orientation, the intellect for a utilitarian adaptation. The intellect by itself is unable to grasp the mysterious aspect of existence and to be moved by it, though it is also an evolved function, mythically speaking: a creation of the Word.

The specific danger threatening the evolution of mankind is precisely that intellectualization may prevail over spiritualization. It is the danger symbolized in the Judaic myth by Adam's sin and in the Greek myth by Prometheus' punishment. It is the same truth expressed in verse 11: though he is a creation of evolution, "created" by the animating impulse mysteriously immanent in the whole of nature, man, when overintellectualized, does not recognize himself as mysteriously animated. Animated beings have become conscious through the progressive incarnation of the spirit, the Word, yet they "do not know him." They forget what is essential in themselves.

VERSE 12

> But to all who did accept him
> he gave power to become children of God.

"All who did accept him" (the Word, the Logos) are the men in whom the vital impulse is strong and who, throughout the centuries, have been moved by the feeling of mystery symbolically called God and for whom this emotion has become motivating, creative of harmony of thought, feeling, and volition; it is the line of essentially animated men whose story is the central theme of the Old Testament.

All these, whether history mentions them or not, are "children of God." Partially animated by essential emotion, they are distinguished by the myth from the "Only Son," the sanctified man.

How could we fail to perceive that the phrase "children of God" is just an image and not a reality, a symbol and, moreover, a symbol known to all mythologies? If this is the case, why should the phrase "Only Son of God" be of another order and be understood literally? Simple respect for the texts, even regardless of any theoretical consideration, should impose an unequivocal translation. Either the theme of divine filiation is to be symbolically understood or, if one takes the Prologue literally, it must be admitted that those who believe in the truly divine filiation of Jesus themselves miraculously receive the same privilege of being actually begotten by a real God.

There is no point giving further proof of what has already been proven. Belief has subconsciously obsessive motivations; its roots are deeply embedded in the magical layer of the psyche as yet insufficiently penetrated, in most men, by progressive intellectualization and spiritualization. The somewhat infantile belief in a Providence that actually watches over each one of us remains the surest support of dogmatic belief.

Obsessive belief may well admit the supernatural and transform it into a dogma; the human spirit that is the most evolved function of nature is such that it cannot, however, do so without falling into the ambivalent anxiety of doubt. Now doubt—like any other anxiety—must seek appeasement by resolving the ambivalent split. Real appeasement can come only from a certainty based on a knowledge that eliminates both the exalted belief and the exalted doubt that is its ambivalent polar opposite. And from where could this certainty come if not from the knowledge of psychic functioning extended to the understanding of its symbolizing function?

VERSE 12 (SECOND PART)

> . . . to all who believe in the name of him,

"The name of God"[20] is a constantly recurring phrase in the Old as well as the New Testament ("hallowed be thy *name*"). ". . . [A]ll who believe in his name" (the name of the Word, therefore the name of God) indicates, like "the children of God," all those who are animated by essential trust in life and by emotion in the face of its unfathomable mystery, feeling as they do the danger of transforming it into an entity superstitiously venerated and implored. They are the men of the Old Covenant who understood the essential truth behind biblical symbolism.

VERSE 13

> Who was born not of human stock
> or urge of flesh,
> or will of man
> but of God himself.

Verse 13 again characterizes this essential humanity previously described as "children of God." It is the symbolism of birth and filiation commonly used by all mythologies.

"Born of human stock or urge of flesh or will of man" here describes human activity as motivated by an excessive attachment to multiple desires. The opposition between the two symbolic modes of filiation is condensed in the juxtaposition of the phrases *"born of will of man"* and *"born of God himself."* What is begotten either by the carnal principle or by the spiritual principle is desire, as is also expressed in a similar formulation "what is born of flesh is flesh/what is born of the Spirit is Spirit" (Jn 3:6). The dual filiation of man is a fundamental mythical theme. It appears in Genesis: Adam is made out of the soil and animated by the breath of God. Here, it is less the intrapsychic conflict of man that is considered than the distinction revealed in the essential history of mankind between men of strong vital impulse and the mass of conventional beings. The men of strong impulse, the "children of God," are not only the exceptional men of the Old Testament, the great characters of Genesis or the prophets, but the anonymous men of good sense who are relatively harmonized and able to resist instinctively the temptations and threats of the environment, the very same people Jesus will call "the salt of the earth."

One should certainly not confuse mythical images with reality, but it is very important also, once the meaning has been uncovered, to free oneself from the persistent suggestive power of the images. God does not exist, the Word does not exist, the beginning does not exist, Christ is not a person, spirit and flesh are not entities. *All these words are only symbols,* "figures of speech," used to express that which alone exists essentially: the capacity of man to be moved, during his ephemeral life, by the unfathomable mystery of life and death, and the specific danger of letting himself be totally captivated by his multiple desires and anxieties. It is the conflict in the human being, symbolized by the duality of spirit and flesh.

This conflictual duality between spirit and flesh is misunderstood by moralizing dogmatism as well as by banalizing atheism, which see in it an invitation to asceticism. The flesh is seen as guilty and the strength of the spirit as lying in its capacity to suppress the desires: this is the fundamental error. The natural function of the spirit, in fact its only function, is to master and organize the material and sexual desires, the desires of the flesh, with the purpose of harmonizing them. "Born of God" or "born of the spirit" means "animated by an essential desire strong enough to let the ideal of harmonization prevail in the inner deliberation of the individual over the attraction of the multiple desires, which, begetting one another without end, end up losing their point of unity and dissolving the essential self, which is *the state of banalization.*" "Born of human stock and urge of flesh," thus denotes the innate weakness of the vital impulse (original sin) that renders individuals incapable of resisting the imaginative exaltation of the contradictory desires invading their psyche.

In this text showing that the *incarnation* of the Word, the spirit, in matter, is the evolutionary process immanent in nature, it is impossible that the ambivalent and ascetic split between exalted spirit and exalted material desires be presented as the ideal goal.

Quite the contrary, complete mastery over earthly desires by the valuating and harmonizing spirit, complete incarnation of the spirit in the flesh, which is the central theme of this text, is condensed and made more specific in the following verse toward which the meaning of the whole Prologue, and beyond this of the whole New Testament, is directed and in which it culminates.

VERSE 14

The Word was made flesh . . .

It is now, and only now, in this third part of the Prologue, that the myth refers to the real man Jesus, the sanctified man whose example (as in another culture the example of Buddha) was suggestive enough to inspire those who had understood it with the courage to oppose the decadent world of their time and to become initiators of a new culture.

Jesus is symbolically designated as the one in whom the Word became incarnate. A sanctified man, purified from the sin of Adam, animated only by his essential desire, by emotion before the mystery and who has attained the imperishable joy that no accident can destroy, he can be called the incarnation of the meaning of life, the incarnation of the Word. The mythical phrase "the Word was made flesh" has a biogenetic meaning and a psychological meaning.

In its biogenetic meaning, it signifies that the sanctified man who has been able totally (though dynamically) to master the blinding affect of the multiple desires and invest all his energy in the essential desire, can be considered as the most evolved form of harmony, as the most perfect achievement of what nature "wants"; the re-creation of more and more complex and intense forms of harmony being the very meaning of evolution.[21]

And indeed, what more perfect image can we find for the meaning of life than that of a human being who has overcome the suffering inherent to life by achieving in himself a complete harmony of thoughts, feelings, and will? To such a degree that this harmonious organization resists, even in its final agony, the opposition and hatred of the world?

From the psychological viewpoint, the incarnation of the spirit is the total penetration of the flesh, of the carnal desires by the spirit.

For spirit, on the human level, is not only organizing, it has become valuating and explanatory. The spirit that fulfills its function ceases to escape from reality, to play imaginatively with the unachievable and the unprovable, and thus becomes an effective guide of activity. The superconscious spirit, when it is no longer clouded by multiple affects, dictates to man what he must do to achieve essential satisfaction: it becomes *incarnate*. The Son (the sanctified man) obeys in all things his Father (the superconscious spirit, his own spirit), as Jesus talking about himself does not cease to affirm. Dogmatic exegesis and symbolic exegesis are radically opposed to each other concerning the interpretation of this verse and hence concerning the myth of the trinity. If one is right, the other is wrong.

For *dogmatic exegesis*, the hope of mankind to overcome suffering depends on the good or ill will of a real God who is really concerned with judging men. Those persons named "Word" and "Holy Spirit" have been at his side since the beginning. Tired of punishing mankind with his anger because of Adam's disobedience, he sends the Word, a real person, really preexistent, who assumes the human form of Jesus, and thus becomes his Son.

For *symbolic exegesis*, God is not a person, but a symbol, created superconsciously by man in order to express his emotion in the face of the unfathomable mystery of life and death. The hope of mankind does not depend on the decisions of a transcendent being, but on *the immanent vital impulse, the evolutionary drive through which the whole of nature frees itself from the dissatisfaction of vital anxiety.*

On the human level, this anxious dissatisfaction is the consequence of vanity. The individualized vital impulse is the fight against vanity and this impulse, when it attains ultimate victory and imperishable joy in an individual, becomes for all mankind a source of hope, pointing toward the evolutionary path, and even a source of faith in life itself since life's meaning—that anxiety can be overcome—is most clearly manifested in the achievement of the sanctified man.

To sum up, this verse can be taken in two ways:

1. For dogma, *Jesus is the Word* made flesh. The Word, conceived from the first verses on as a real person, decides to take on a real body.

2. For symbolic exegesis, Jesus is *the Word become flesh*. Jesus is considered by the myth as the incarnation of the meaning of life symbolically called the Word.[22]

VERSE 14 (THIRD PART)

> . . . he lived among us,
> and we saw his glory,
> the glory that is his as the only Son of the Father,
> full of grace and truth.

Here we see the fundamental theme of divine filiation and especially the expression "Only Son" of the Father, therefore the third person of the symbolic trinity (second person of the dogmatic trinity).

Now there are many passages in the Gospels, as we know, in which Jesus is symbolically called "Son of God." However, there is a very important distinction between the two meanings of this mythical image: either it is used to metaphorically characterize the man Jesus, or it is used to denote the third person of the symbolic trinity, as is the case here.

In the Gospels, the man Jesus talks about himself as "Son of God," "sent by the Father," doing the will of the Father and not his own. The witnesses address him as "Son of God." In this context, the expression is metaphorical and has above all an ethical meaning; it is in perfect conformity with the flowery language still common nowadays in the Middle East. It means, "I behave 'as if' I were the son of God," "it is the divine in me that motivates my actions, my thoughts and my will." Jesus is entirely animated by the essential desire (only son) and not only partially so, as are the many "children of God" (verse 12), for whom the ideal is a goal that they cannot fully achieve. Jesus is the achievement of the ethical ideal, and this is what his contemporaries (at least a small number of them) understood when they recognized him as the Son of God. None of them mistook him for a miraculously conceived man-god. On the other hand, they often misunderstood the universal scope of his message and saw in him the one who was going to reinstate Israel in its temporal power.

However, it is essential to take into account the fact that the Prologue of John's Gospel is different from the other gospel texts in that it deals only secondarily with the man Jesus and his accomplishment (which is the theme of the other Gospels) and is mostly concerned with the phenomenon of sanctification[23] considered as an integral part of the evolutionary process of life. Being the conscious achievement of the ideal of harmonization that is immanent in existence, it thereby enlightens the whole meaning and direction of evolution.

Thus the phrase "Only Son of the Father," used in the Prologue, goes beyond the solitary achievement of the man Jesus. The Only Son,[24] no longer in the metaphorical meaning of the term, but in its deeply significant symbolic content, is the essence of this achievement; victory over suffering brought into this world by "the sin of Adam" having been achieved once in history, its reenactment throughout the ages is for mankind the only hope of satisfaction.

The myth of the incarnation is not merely a testimony about Jesus, it is a testimony about the fact that a decisive stage of evolution has been reached and that the result is a great hope for all mankind. Moreover, it shows that the achievement of the most evolved man enlightens all men and enables them to grasp the meaning and direction of life, the past and the future of evolution. Symbolically speaking, the achievement of the ideal on the human level "reveals" in its entirety "God's design," the immanent meaning of life, ignorance of which is a source of disorientation ("wandering in the darkness"). The trinitarian myth, in its widest meaning, is summed up in the last verse of the Prologue:

> No one has ever seen God,
> it is the Only Son, who is nearest to the Father's heart
> who has made him known.

What we have analyzed is the deepest meaning of the Prologue. It does not prevent this text, as we have said, from having its *raison d'être* in the example of the man Jesus, and indeed Jesus in person is present from verse 14 onward.

In short, there are two fundamental distinctions to be made in order to grasp the real meaning of the Prologue. On the one hand, one must clearly distinguish *Jesus*, the historical person, from the *Word*, a mythical symbol. The central affirmation of the Prologue "the Word was made flesh" is *symbolic* and refers to the existence of a *real* man, emphasizing the evolutionary significance of his achievement. It is not the proclamation of a miraculous event. It adds to the real hero the dimension of a mythical hero, thereby showing that the truth he incarnates is the same that is present in all myths and in the Hebrew myth in particular, from which stems the entire New Testament. On the other hand, one must distinguish the man Jesus from the mythical *Son* of God, or Only Son, a symbol of the evolutionary hope included in the achievement of Jesus. This achievement is thus linked to the meaning immanent in life "from the beginning" since it appears as its outcome and its clarification and it is also linked to the future of evolution of which it appears as the prefiguration. Thus in the symbolic trinity Father, Word, and Son, the third person is not Jesus, but the symbolic Son, the evolutionary hope of mankind prefigured by the achievement of Jesus. This latter distinction is the same as the one to be made between Jesus and *Christ* (a word that does not appear until verse 17), which is, like "Son," a symbolic image. "Christ," the central symbol of the New Testament, is borrowed from the Old Testament. It is the Greek translation of the Hebrew word *Messiah*, which means "Anointed."

The Anointed of the Lord or Messiah of the Old Testament is not a present or future person, but the truth that is superconsciously known by all men and that, through evolutionary necessity, has to become incarnate and motivating in all men, the only condition for justice to rule on earth.

The Christ of the New Testament is the fulfillment of the ancestral hope of seeing the superconsciously known truth verified and actualized. Jesus is symbolically the Christ because he has attained the ideal whose relative achievement is the responsibility of every man. But the existence of Jesus does not *achieve*, contrary to what dogmatism pretends (and history cruelly disproves), the hope of mankind. His achievement, symbolically called *Christ*, shows the *possibility* and thus strengthens the *hope* that the suffering that rules because of the greed of desires can be overcome through evolution. Jesus is the Christ, but he is only, to use the expression of the apostle Paul, "the first fruits" of the complete incarnation of the truth in the thinking species. In this sense, he is "the Son," the bearer of hope. "Christ" is the ethical achievement, the Son is the evolutionary hope.

Verse 14 continues as follows: "He lived among us [literally, "he pitched his tent among us"] and we saw his glory. . . ." The *tent* is a symbol that appears quite frequently in the Bible. A memory of ancestral nomadism, it is protection and shelter. Therefore it symbolizes that which essentially protects man; i.e., his valuations. The "tent" pitched by Christ in the world is a refuge for the disoriented souls who understand his message. Verse 14 can be compared to a passage from Paul's Epistles (2 Cor 12:9) ". . . so that the power of Christ may stay [literally, "pitch his tent"] over me. . . ." The tent also symbolizes the detachment, the simplicity of Jesus' way of life.

"And we saw his glory" is interpreted by dogmatism as the testimony of eyewitnesses who had seen the supernatural phenomena that would have marked the passage on earth of the man-God: the miracles,[25] the actual Resurrection and Ascension. Thought, when it loses the methodological certainty that alone can distinguish between the possible and the impossible, can keep a pseudological structure while losing itself in absurdity. The epistemological basis of thought lies in the distinction between mystery and appearance, and the fundamental methodological rule of scientific thought lies in bringing neither existing modalities into mystery nor mystery into modalities.

In keeping with the meaning of the verses that have been deciphered so far, the phrase means that the disciples of Jesus have grasped the scope of his example, the achievement that makes him truly worthy of the title "glory" of mankind. They have, more essentially, seen the "glory," the splendor of the universal and fecundating truth that is symbolically called Christ.

The "Only Son" symbol has already been translated; as to "grace" ("full of grace and truth"), which is interpreted by theological dogmatism as the miraculous gift bestowed on human beings by a real and transcendent God, it is indeed a gift but the unexplainable and unmerited (gracious) gift of life and of vital impulse that, through its own evolutionary dynamics (to use psychological terms, through the strength of its sublime calculus of satisfaction), can create complete harmony in the human psyche, faith in life, joy in life.

VERSE 16

> Indeed from his fullness we have, all of us, received yes, grace in return for grace.[26]

Through our removal of verse 15, this verse follows quite naturally on verse 14.

Grace is most certainly the gift of life, but this gift is lost if one does not have the capacity to receive it, to merit it. In this sense, grace is the enlightenment of the soul and spirit, the power of the vital impulse capable of overcoming the torment of anxiety extending over past and future. The soul, shriveled and blinded by the egocentric affect of multiple desires, becomes objective when man experiences himself as mysteriously animated, as an attempt by nature to break through toward essential satisfaction. Grace is the gift of life received and accepted: responsibility fully accepted in the face of the mysteriously immanent meaning of life.

Whoever lives in such a way, without guilty vanity or accusing complaint, entirely animated by the evolutionary impulse that kindles, "lights up" preconscious life and enlightens conscious life, is "full of grace and truth" and becomes for others a vivifying example, a bearer of grace, a source of grace.

VERSE 17

> Since, though the Law was given through Moses,
> grace and truth have come through Jesus Christ.

This verse unites and at the same time contrasts the deep significances of the Old and the New Testament, of the Old Covenant and the New Covenant.[27]

The truth has always been known. It has always been expressed anew by the myths of all peoples, in its two essential aspects: metaphysical truth, which is the radical and definitive distinction between the unfathomable mystery of the Origins and manifest appearance; ethical truth, which is the immanent call to harmonization given effect by immanent justice. The life of cultures depends on the importance of the response to this truth in the souls of individuals. Decadence sets in with the growing disorientation bred by oblivion of the essential truth.

Truth cannot be completely incarnate in individuals, it has to be *suggested*. This is the task of the priestly class during the periods when culture is flourishing, when the veracious suggestion based on myth finds an echo in the souls of individuals.

With the progress of intellectualization, suggestion—which is at first magical, then mythical—can become conceptual formulation. This is what happened with the Law of Moses. But so long as truth is not incarnate, as long as it is not imposed on the individual by his own superconscious, it always runs the risk of being degraded into magical suggestion or verbal impositions; i.e., into moralism, which will never cease to be fought by growing immoralism.

The santified man does not obey the law, he obeys his own superconscious. He is a law unto himself, he incarnates the immutable law of harmony ruling all that exists. He does not want to impose a new law—to judge the world—but to free man from the law (though it is a historical necessity); i.e., to save the world. Neither does he ask man to follow him on the way toward sanctification. He shows that everyone can, according to his own strength, find essential satisfaction if—rejecting all precepts—he listens to the call of his own superconscious, even though he be the only one to do so in the midst of a disoriented world. His example makes the law, the collective guide of a people, obsolete and brings "grace and truth": the possible awakening in every human psyche of the evolutionary impulse (Word and Light) incarnate in all of nature, but stifled in the human being by the imaginative exaltation of desires and by inhibiting anxiety.

VERSE 18

> No one has ever seen God,
> it is the Only Son, who is nearest to the Father's heart,
> who has made him known.

Thus the mythical tale of the incarnation goes back to its origin. It strongly reaffirms the mythical foundation of all cultures, more central and more explicit in the Judeo-Christian myth than in all others: God is the forever unfathomable mystery. He makes himself known only through the Word, the evolutionary impulse, whose clearest manifestation is the truth incarnate in man, the Only Son. The Son, "visible image of the invisible God," as the apostle Paul puts it, the fully accomplished vital impulse, motivated by emotion inspired by mystery, is symbolically speaking, *"near the heart"* of God mystery. The Son did not make known the real nature of God in the sense of dogma, because nothing can make it known.[28] Who would dare say that he knows God, without being struck by the blasphemous absurdity of such an assertion? Yet this is what people affirm when they claim that Jesus, a God-man, an integral part of the deity, reveals the divine nature to those who are incorporated into the Church by the magic of the rites. How much deeper is the mythical truth. The Only Son, transcending the example of the man Jesus, is the evolutionary hope of all mankind, insofar as mankind is heir to the only truth, experienced by one man and thereby become the hope of all men. Through this possibility given to mankind to overcome the suffering due to intellectualization (the sin of Adam), the design of God "is made known": the evolutionary future of the thinking species is clarified; i.e., the incarnation in mankind of the eternal and only truth called Christ.

Here ends our deciphering of the symbolism in the Prologue. It will be followed by a translation of the symbolic meaning of the first verses of the Gospel proper, namely verses 6, 7, 8, 9, and 15 of the traditional text of the Prologue.

If the Prologue of the Gospel of John can be called a cosmic vision of evolution and a foreshadowing of the essential future of mankind, the Gospel itself (which starts after verse 18) can be called a testimony for Jesus Christ.

That is to say that the Evangelist is not so much concerned with an account of the life of Jesus (and still less, with the proof that his origin and destiny were supernatural) as with showing that *Jesus is the Christ*, not in realistic terms, but symbolically so.

VERSE 6

A man came, sent by God.
His name was John.

The Gospel itself starts with the testimony of John the Baptist. The scope of this testimony of John the Baptist is much greater than that of a historical anecdote, not because—as dogma would have it—John was the predestined annunciator of the miracle, but because he symbolizes and sums up the prophetic spirit of the Old Testament, and at the same time ushers in the New

Covenant; i.e., a new expression, fuller and more universal, of the eternal truth.

VERSE 7

> He came as a witness,
> as a witness to speak for the light,
> so that everyone might believe through him.

John the Baptist is introduced as *a witness for the light*. Now the light, as we have seen in analyzing verse 5 ("a light that shines in the dark, a light that darkness could not overpower") is the truth superconsciously known by human beings and that the subconscious cannot entirely repress. All the prophets were witnesses for the light, men of strong vital impulse, lucid as to their own motivations and animated by a desire to enlighten others, to help men tear themselves away from banalization.

John the Baptist is of the same stock as all those who have been "witnesses for the light" throughout history, since he too was symbolically *sent* by God *so that* everyone might believe through him. These seemingly finalistic expressions are used by literal dogmatism to assert that the vocation of John the Baptist, like that of the Old Testament prophets, was actually the result of divine will, that it was an element of a truly preestablished divine plan.

John the Baptist was not *sent by God in order* to testify for Jesus Christ, nor was he sent *so that* everyone might believe through him. He was animated by his own vital impulse.

The finalism of the phrase is symbolic and expresses this inner need driving John to support the preaching of the one with whom he felt a spiritual affinity, while recognizing and publicly affirming the superiority of the sanctified man ("I am not fit to undo his sandal strap"—Jn 1:27).

Finalistic language such as "so that . . . ," "in order that . . ." is in perfect conformity with the spirit of mythical symbolism. The "will" of God, the " design " of God, are common symbolic formulations through which the myth expresses the mysterious and lawful intentionality ruling all phenomena of the outer and the inner world.

The fact that the history of mankind is periodically punctuated by the appearance of men who are animated by an exceptional vital impulse can be explained without invoking a supernatural predestination. From the dawn of life on earth, the prime mover of evolution has been anxious dissatisfaction seeking its satisfying appeasement.[29]

Eras of decadence, such as the Roman empire, such as our own, are characterized by an anxious disorientation with respect to ethical values, cynically denied, or superstitiously hypostatized. Such an anxious disorientation has always, in the course of history, brought about a renewal of reflection on the meaning of life. In a few rare individuals, suffering gives rise to a renewed upsurge of their strength of soul and spirit, of the evolutionary impulse with which they oppose the prevailing disorientation by reasserting again and again the immanence of values that is symbolically called wisdom and will of God, or Word of God, or Light.

In psychological terms, the phenomenon of prophecy, the theme of the Old Testament, summed up in the first chapter of John's Gospel, and the phenomenon of sanctification, the theme of the New Testament, are evolutionary phenomena that—in line with the constant process of mythical language—appear in the Bible "as if" the transcendental "will" of "God" had brought them about.

VERSE 8

> He was not the light,
> only a witness to speak for the light.

As we have already explained, the symbol "light" has two complementary meanings. The light of verse 5 is truth in general; the light John the Baptist speaks for is still truth in general but it also becomes the truth that Jesus incarnates and proclaims anew.

John the Baptist "is not the light" because he is not Christ: he is not totally motivated by the essential truth or light. But if he had not been "witness for the light" in general—i.e., capable of discerning essential truth from essential error—he could not have been "witness for the light coming into the world": for the truth brought by Jesus, for Christ.

VERSE 9

> The Word was the true light
> that enlightens all men;
> and he was coming into the world.

This light is the new formulation of the truth, which is all the more "enlightening" since it appears in "the dark" of a decadent era. *The light is not Jesus, the light is Christ*, the truth already announced in the Old Testament, incarnate, actualized, made active force and elucidating thought through the personal achievement of the man Jesus, who can therefore be symbolically called Jesus-Christ, the man animated by faith in the essence of life, capable of emotion in the face of the mysterious depths of existence and its manifest harmony.

It is certainly impossible to separate radically the living man and his message. Jesus says about himself: "I, the light, have come into the world" (Jn 12:46). But before this assertion, there comes a fundamental distinction, voiced by Jesus himself:

JN 12:44–45

> Whoever believes in me,
> believes *not in me*,
> but in *the one who sent me*,
> and whoever sees me,
> sees the one who sent me.

"The one who sent me" just as the one who "sent" John the Baptist (verse 6) is the superconscious spirit, his own vital impulse compelling him to harmonize himself. In order to become harmonized, enlightened by vivifying faith, man must free himself from the imaginative exaltation of desires and their obsessive avidity. The clarification of the meaning of life proceeds from man's clarification of his own motives: from lucidity with respect to himself. Superconscious light must become conscious enlightenment opposed to the darkness of the subconscious. The light is thus above all the truth about man, the veracity of his own self-judgment as it appears in many passages of the New Testament:

JN 3:19–21

> On this ground is sentence pronounced:
> that though the light has come into the world
> men have shown they prefer
> darkness to light
> because their deeds were evil.
> And, indeed, everybody who does wrong
> hates the light and avoids it,
> for fear his actions should be exposed;
> but the man who lives by the truth
> comes out into the light,
> so that it may be plainly seen that what he does is done in God.

This is an affirmation of man's solitary responsibility before the ethical law. In this sense, as it is written in verse 9, "the light, *the true light enlightens all men*, and he was coming into the world." The message of Jesus concerns all men. What is of fundamental importance for mankind is the message itself and not the fact that it was formulated and achieved by the man Jesus. The historical Jesus passed away like all men, but his message and his exemplary achievement remain eternally.

The apostle Paul was the one who understood best that the truth incarnate in Jesus does not only concern the symbolically chosen people, but all mankind.

VERSE 15

> John appears as his witness (thus as a witness to the Word that
> is the true light).
> He proclaims:
> "This is the one of whom I said:
> He who comes after me
> ranks before me
> because he existed before me."

"He proclaims" stresses emphatically—as does the original Greek text—the persistence of the prophetic voice. Here it is symbolized by John the Baptist, but it is the same voice that has been heard throughout the ages. He refers here to Isaiah, the voice in the wilderness (of the banalized world) and thus appears as the last prophet of the Old Covenant, summing up the entire prophetic message that bears witness to the light.

John the Baptist's declaration, "He who comes after me," etc., is used by theological dogmatism to support its assertions on the dual nature of the *man* Jesus: *divine and human.* "He who comes after me" is the man-god, Jesus-Christ. "He who existed before me" is the Word, a divine person actually preexistent since the beginning. In fact, John the Baptist's exclamation, though rather enigmatic in its form, can be understood if one takes the trouble to distinguish clearly the planes of symbolism and historical reality, which is after all a principle of methodology valid for the deciphering of all biblical texts. "He who comes after" John the Baptist in time is Jesus, whose preaching follows that of John the Baptist. He who "comes before me" refers to Christ, a symbol, not a reality. The essential truth has always existed. It is expressed in symbolic terms by the myths of all peoples. It always existed in the soul of human beings, in the form of an ethical conscience that turns into guiltiness when man does not listen to its evolutionary call. But it had never been incarnate, lived to such a degree by a man in whom it became the sole motivating force.

"He existed before me." This again refers to the symbol Christ. If the truth existed in the historical conscience of mankind it is because it *existed** *essentially*; it is not linked to accidental phenomena, it is the manifestation in the human psyche of the law of harmony that mysteriously rules, since the beginning, the evolutionary interaction between organizing spirit and organized matter.

Thus John the Baptist appears in the Gospel of John as heir to the Judaic culture, the "just man," to use the words of the Old Testament. He is the man who is sufficiently purified in his motives to recognize in Jesus, *the Christ*, the man freed from "the sin" of Adam, he who achieves the age-old hope of mankind. Therefore John the Baptist ushers in a new culture, a universal culture in which the individual, liberated from the forms that are peculiar to any particular religion, can hope, by developing his own vital impulse, to overcome the anxiety of disorientation.

---

*The Greek would be better translated by "was" than by "existed."

This hope, stifled since the dawn of Christianity by dogmatizing error, perdures, however, and finds support and confirmation in the understanding of the true but symbolically veiled significance of the myth of the incarnation. In the last analysis, the fulfillment of this hope depends on the introspective method capable of studying the psychic functioning down to the extra-conscious depths where symbolic language is elaborated.

Part 2

ILLUSTRATIVE EPISODES

CHAPTER 5

John the Baptist

The Gospel of John progressively develops a single symbolic theme. To understand the latter is to be able to understand the symbolism of the Christian myth that had already been expressed in the Prologue and is repeated all through the Johannine Gospel. This theme can be summed up as follows: through the life of the man Jesus, the meaning of life becomes manifest. The organizing harmony that underlies every phenomenon in the existing world then becomes clear, for it is manifested not only at the level of nature, but at the human level. The true faith to which Jesus refers ("If you do not believe that . . .") consists in understanding that all the activities of Jesus—words and deeds—are a tangible manifestation of the meaning of life, harmony. His words express truth and his deeds, goodness. "To see me is to see the Father," Jesus says. This means that he who understands, who sees with the eye of the spirit, the real personality of the man Jesus, truly grasps what he represents: the manifestation on the human plane, of the meaning of life; and, if images are used, the manifestation of the "Father," symbol of the evolutionary superconscious.

Men who are animated by true faith, by enthusiasm for essential life lived at its highest degree by the sanctified man, become themselves capable of expressing in their words and deeds the meaning of life: truth and goodness; they become during their lifetime manifest expressions of harmony. Thus they know inner joy, symbolized by the "kingdom of heaven."

The teaching of Jesus, developed in the form of a dialogue with the Pharisees, is interrupted by episodes that are often symbolically miraculous and that contain the same hidden meaning as his teaching. Such episodes are therefore a concrete illustration of the fundamental meaning contained in all four Gospels. Before studying the symbolic teaching, we will group the illustrative scenes and analyze them in detail.

Before we begin, we should mention that certain verses will not be translated, either because their significance is purely anecdotal (the comings and goings of Jesus and his disciples) or because they are repetitive, or because they have already been translated in previous chapters.

The Gospel starts with the testimony of John the Baptist. Having known Jesus very well since his childhood, John, whose spiritual foresight is tremendous, is fully aware of the uncontestable superiority of Jesus. This is expressed in his testimony. Questioned by the Levites, he replies that he is not the Messiah, the Anointed of the Lord, nor is he Elijah—the prophet who, according to the Bible (2 Kgs 2) ascends to heaven on a chariot of fire and is due to come back to earth—nor yet the new prophet expected at that time. John the Baptist is clearly impelled by his humility, since he is a great prophet as Jesus himself testifies (Mt 11:14).

> 1:19 . . . When the Jews sent priests and Levites from Jerusalem to ask him:
> 1:22 "Who are you . . . what have you to say about yourself?"
> 1:23 So John said: "I am, as Isaiah prophesized:
> a voice that cries in the wilderness: make a straight way for the Lord."

The desert symbolizes the world of banalization where life becomes impoverished, the world where feelings crumble, wills are dissolved like the sands in the desert, shapeless and unstable.

John is therefore the one who, in this banalized world of Roman decadence, cries with all the daring and strength of the Old Testament prophets, and calls everyone to become open to the essential, receptive to an offer of life that rejects banalization, rejects the flattening of the spirit in conventional superstition.

1:24 Now these men had been sent by the Pharisees

1:25 and they put this further question to him: "Why are
you baptizing if you are not the Christ, and not
Elijah, and not the prophet?"

1:26 John replied: "I baptize with water. But there stands
among you—unknown to you—

1:27 the one who is coming after me; and I am not fit to
undo his sandal strap."

Baptism in water is a ritual symbolizing the inner rebirth that must take place in each one of us, the elimination of the old Adam, the old man, as the apostle Paul will say (see the translation of the epistles of Paul;[30] the old Adam is simply man's propensity to exalt his desires). The Pharisees, who are going to become during Jesus' public life his relentless enemies, do not—since they are as far as anyone can be from genuine essential life—know him who in time comes after John, yet who is so tremendously superior to him in sublimating force.

1:29 The next day, seeing Jesus coming toward him, John said: "Look, there is the lamb of God that takes away the sin of the world."

Jesus is symbolically the lamb of God, purity incarnate. In the mythical symbolism of all cultures, the lamb[31] represents, not humility, sweetness, and resignation—as hagiography has claimed—but purity, the lamb offered in sacrifice being always spotless. The Hebrew phrase *Seh tamim* means the lamb without defect, irreproachable, pure, a linguistic expression that is now synonymous with innocence and purity. The sacrifice of the lamb was the assurance given to the divinity of one's purity of intentions. The sacrifice of the pig was the surrender to the divinity of impure desires. The symbolic meaning of the lamb is identical to that of the ram in Greek mythology (image of the Golden Fleece), in Hebrew mythology (sacrifice of Isaac), and in many other episodes. Jesus is neither humble nor resigned, he is proud and combative; it is only in such a view that we can understand the meaning of the strength of his love, which is understanding indulgence rather than sweetness. Being a purified man, he shows to other men, through his example, that it is possible to be purified; he frees in principle and potentially all mankind, the human world, of its weakness, of its "sins," since he, man among

men, is capable of overcoming the weakness inherent in mankind: exaltation of the desires (see the Introduction).

To put it another way, the world is not totally sinful since the
"lamb of God," the being capable of purifying himself of exalted
desires, exists and manifests himself.

> 1:30 This is the one I spoke of when I said: "a man is coming after me
> who ranks before me because he existed before me."

In time, Jesus manifested himself after John, but he is greater
than John, as we have just said, in strength of spirit, because he
embodies the force of sublimation, the essential vital impulse
that has always existed, and goes down the centuries but unveils
itself in a unique way through this man who is unique in his
capacity for essential achievement. Jesus is called the "Only Son"
of God. We must stress that Buddha, in a way that is quite as
unique, also assumes the meaning of life, the sublimation of exalted desires. This does not contradict what we have said before.
Here are two cycles of cultures, each of which gave birth to its
own unique hero; this adjective is meant to show the radical
difference between the victorious hero—Jesus or Buddha—and
other men; and on the other hand, to express the inner unity
lived by him, in contradiction to the duality splitting all other
men in various degrees.

> 1:31 I did not know him myself, and yet, it was to reveal him to
> Israel that I came baptizing with water.

On the plane of reality, John knew Jesus because he was his
cousin. But he did not know the degree of intensity that could
be attained by the sublimating force of the spirit, incarnate in the
man Jesus and manifested through his words and deeds.

Offering to men baptism with water, John wanted to prepare
them to "be reborn," to receive the word of Jesus, his message.
This "baptism of water" is a ritual receiving its significance only
if it is accompanied by an inner disposition making man receptive to the message of Jesus. The rite of baptism means "the
death of the old Adam" (Adam being the symbol of the exalted
attachment to earthly desires). Immersed in water, man comes
up renewed.

> 1:32 I saw the Spirit coming down on him from heaven like a
> dove and resting on him.

John, seeing Jesus, had a revelation, not in a miraculous or magical sense, as we have already explained, but in the commonly used meaning of the term; he understood intuitively, he felt the total strength of the spirit dwelling in that man. This strength of the spirit is symbolized by the dove. In all myths, the bird—in its positive significance—symbolizes the sublime flight of the spirit (see the Introduction).

In the dogmatic conception, the dove is the Holy Spirit, the third person of the trinity, a kind of independent entity without any material substance, sent by a real God to his real Son. Now the holy spirit is the symbol for the spirit that organizes matter in all apparent phenomena; being an evolutionary phenomenon, it ends up by animating living matter until it becomes, at the human level, the spirit that valuates desires and explains the world.

It is not the third person of the trinitarian myth, but the second person, since 2 is the number of the appearance as a whole.[32]

> 1:33 I did not know him myself, but he who sent me to baptize
> with water had said to me: "The man on whom you see
> the Spirit come down and rest is the one who is going
> to baptize with the Holy Spirit."
> 1:34 Yes, I have seen and I am the witness that he is the Chosen
> one of God.

For John, the "[one] who sent [him] to baptize with water" is his own vital impulse. The one who appears to him as having an exceptional strength of spirit, Jesus, appears to him quite obviously capable not only of reawakening in man the intention of "being reborn" to essential life, of finding again the meaning of life, but also of making possible the achievement of such a rebirth. The intention of rebirth is symbolized by the "baptism with the Holy Spirit." Jesus can awaken from their essential sleep men who are capable of understanding him, he can make them be born again to the genuine life of the spirit, the miracle can take place. John is certain of this. Because he has seen, thanks to his exceptional vital impulse, the strength of soul dwelling in the man Jesus.

The First Disciples of Jesus

1:35 On the following day as John stood there with two
of his disciples,
1:36 Jesus passed, and John stared hard at him and said: "Look,
there is the lamb of God."
1:37 Hearing this, the two disciples followed Jesus.
1:38 Jesus turned around, saw them following and said: "What do
you want?" They answered: "Rabbi—which means Teacher—
where do you live?"
1:39 "Come and see," he replied.

The two disciples ask Jesus, "What is your way of life? Do
you live in the essential, do you live only according to the essential?" To which Jesus answers, "See what I am, see how I live,
listen to what I offer and you will know."

1:39 So they went and saw where he lived, and stayed with him the
rest of the day. It was about the tenth hour.

They too, like John, are convinced by the essential strength
emanating from this man, they have seen where he "lived," he
"lives" in the essential, and this compels them to stay with Jesus.
Ten is the number of fulfillment.

1:40 One of these two who became the followers of Jesus after hearing
what John had said, was Andrew, the brother of Simon Peter.
1:41 Early next morning, Andrew met his brother and said to him:
"We have found the Messiah—which means the Christ."

The Messiah means Christ in Aramaic, and Christ is the
Anointed of the Lord.

1:42 and he took Simon to Jesus. Jesus looked hard at him and said: "You are Simon, son of John; you are to be called Cephas, meaning Rock."

Jesus was impressed by Simon; the name he gives him signifies the strength of character he feels in him, solid as a rock. This aspect of Simon Peter's character will be stressed again when Jesus will tell him, "You are Peter and on this rock, I will build my Church," which means "The community of my disciples will be made of men whose faith is as strong as yours."

1:43 The next day, after Jesus had decided to leave for Galilee, he met Philip and said: "Follow me."
1:44 Philip came from the same town, Bethsaida, as Andrew and Peter.
1:45 Philip found Nathanael and said to him: "We have found the one Moses wrote about in the Law, the one about whom the prophets wrote. He is Jesus, son of Joseph, from Nazareth."
1:46 "From Nazareth?" said Nathanael, "can anything good come from that place?" "Come and see", replied Philip.
1:47 When Jesus saw Nathanael coming, he said of him, "This is an Israelite who deserves the name, incapable of deceit."

"Here is a man capable of honesty, he does not lie to himself, he has the vital impulse of going beyond himself."

1:48 "How do you know me?" said Nathanael. "Before Philip came to call you," said Jesus, "I saw you under the fig tree."

Thus Jesus tells him, "Even before you were invited by Philip to come to me calling you to the essential, I saw that you had a vital impulse, a yearning for essential life, that you could be reached."

The fig tree is the symbol—as are all trees—of the vital impulse and of the satisfying consequences it brings (fruits). The tree is rooted in the earth just as the vital impulse is rooted in earthly desires, it grows vertically toward the sky like the impulse, which rises as it develops.

1:49 Nathanael answered: "Rabbi, you are the Son of God, you are the King of Israel!"

In the symbolic significance we have just shown, it is understandable that Nathanael, moved by the fact that Jesus had foreknown his impulse toward the essential, replies to him:

"Rabbi, you are the incarnation of the essential, all your being manifests the organizing harmony, you are the symbolic son of God."

1:50 Jesus replied: "You believe that just because I said: I saw you under the fig tree. You will see greater things than that."

1:51 And then he added: "I tell you most solemnly, you will see heaven laid open, and, above the Son of Man, the angels of God ascending and descending."

What the disciples of Jesus will see and what is still better than the simple intuition of Jesus regarding the people who open themselves to him, is the heaven of joy.

The open sky is the symbol of inner joy, due to certainty regarding the meaning of life; such a certainty will develop in the spirit of the disciples; they will become able to understand the sublime thoughts (angels) animating the Son of Man; thus they will share with him joy and certainty (cf. 16:23,26).

The "angels"—a word that in literal translation means "messenger"—are what emanates from God; i.e., Jesus' superconscious. A deliberating dynamics is thus established between his superconscious and his conscious, symbolized by the ascent and descent of the sublime valuations. The same image is found in the Old Testament in the dream of Jacob (Gen 28:12).

CHAPTER 7

The Wedding at Cana;
The Cleansing of the Temple

The testimony of John is followed by the first two acts in Jesus' public life: the miracle at the Wedding at Cana, and the intervention in the Temple when he drives out the merchants.

These two facts mark the beginning of his public life and sum up symbolically the fundamental meaning of his mission. The miracle at Cana, if it is literally understood, would only be an act of bragging and would have no other purpose than getting people drunk after they had already imbibed; the intervention in the Temple, if it were literally understood, would only be the madness of an exalted man.

In the Christian myth, the image of wine is used in its positive significance; it symbolizes blood, itself a symbol of the soul and its specific expression: love for the essential. Symbolically speaking, water can be a positive spirit, truth flowing from the source, but then it would not be counter to wine. At Cana, water in contrast to wine therefore has a negative significance; it is, in contrast to wine, tasteless, it symbolizes the platitude of the spirit. Thus the people at the wedding are animated by banal spirit (water), which will be transformed into spiritual enthusiasm (wine).[33]

Before starting his public mission, Jesus talks to this close circle of friends and awakens the sleeping spirit of those who gathered for banal festivities.

Here is the translation, verse by verse:

2:3 When they ran out of wine, since the wine provided for the wedding was all finished, the mother of Jesus said to him: "They have no wine."

There is no wine, which therefore means that the guests are more or less devoid of this sublime enthusiasm, this appetite for truth, which are the expression of the essential vital impulse, of "the soul."

2:4 Jesus said:
"Woman, why turn to me? My hour has not yet come."

Mary, his mother, would like to push him to bring the essential food to the guests at the wedding; she would therefore want him to speak. But Jesus guesses that the motive of his mother, while being maternal love, is also pride in her son; she would like him to be admired. If he decides to talk, the motive is quite different: a sublime motive, significant for all his future mission. It is therefore important to show as clearly as possible the difference between the two motives. Although Mary's motive is quite understandable for a mother, it would be quite unforgivable for Jesus. His response to his mother's request shows quite clearly the difference between their motives: "What do you want to push me to do? I am not inclined to do it." Or, according to other translations, "Woman, what is there between you and me?" "What is common to my motive and your motive?"

2:6 There were six stone jars standing there, meant for the ablutions that are customary among the Jews; each could hold twenty or thirty gallons.
2:7 Jesus said to the servants: "Fill the jars with water," and they filled them to the brim.

As a purification ritual, the use of this water is nothing but a convention. Jesus places them in front of the reality of their practices: "This is what you are doing: your receptivity (the jars) is filled only with tasteless moralizing conventions (water)." He will struggle all his life against these moralizing conventions, which are the source of an essential death.

2:8 "Draw some out now," he told them, "and take it to the steward." They did this.
2:9 The steward tasted the water and it had turned into wine. Having no idea where it came from—only the servants who had drawn the water knew—the steward called the bridegroom.

The water is thus turned into wine. The tasteless moralizing conventions are, thanks to the word that Jesus brings to his listeners, replaced by the food of the soul, capable of awakening spiritual enthusiasm. The man Jesus, through his teaching, gives himself without holding anything back, offering his soul (wine) and awakening the soul of those who listen from conventional sleep. The "miracle" at Cana, preceding the public mission, is thus a parallel to the Last Supper, which brings that mission to an end; the Last Supper is a meal in the close circle of the Apostles, in which—according to the Synoptic Gospels—he gives wine to drink: he offers his blood, his soul, to feed the soul of his disciples.

The episode in which he drives out the merchants of the Temple has the same significance as that of the Wedding at Cana. The difference is that it no longer takes place in a small circle; it sums up the future mission and the stance of Jesus who is fearless and undaunted by the world. According to learned sources, the money-changers and merchants of cattle and pigeons for the sacrifice were not admitted into the sanctuary, and not even into the outer courts. It is possible that at the time of Jesus, a time of decadence and laxity of mores, they may have been tolerated in the outer area of the Temple. In any event, the merchants have a symbolic significance, they are here the "merchants" of superstitions, priests and Pharisees who profane sublime life, essential life symbolized by the Temple. They symbolize banality, essential death of the soul that Jesus must chase away so that the Temple of life, essential life, not be defiled anymore.

Here is the verse-by-verse translation:

2:13 Just before the Jewish Passover, Jesus went up to Jerusalem.
2:14 And in the Temple, he found people selling cattle and sheep and pigeons, and the money-changers sitting at their counters there.
2:15 Making a whip out of some cord, he drove them all out of the Temple, cattle and sheep as well, scattered the money-changers' coins, knocked their tables over.

The whip here is the tool with which he scourges their mercantile souls, the word with which he attacks them. Jesus' virulent attack is thus verbal, as the translation shows. An attack with a whip would have simply led people to see Jesus as a dangerous madman, and he would have immediately been arrested. Note, by the way, that this forceful attack by Jesus shows how the man who dares to oppose the most rooted conventions is not the sweet Jesus, the sentimental hero he became in the minds of Christians, misunderstanding his true dimension.

The tables of the money-changers and their coins symbolize the tables of false values and their false promises of satisfaction, which must be overthrown and replaced by genuine values: faith in the essential and love of life. But if the Temple symbolically means essential life, it is in fact the place where superstition is flaunted. Really driving the profaners out of the Temple would even serve no useful purpose: the symbolic Temple would still be polluted by them. Those who should watch over the purity of the Temple—the Pharisees—profane it themselves by their superstition. They want to forbid Jesus to intervene in what they believe is their duty and their right: the problem of values. They ask Jesus to prove by a sign, a prodigy, a miracle, the right he has to interfere in the "purification of the Temple"; i.e, his authority for teaching what goes against their belief turned into superstition.

> 2:18 The Jews intervened and said: "What sign can you show us
> to justify what you have done?"
> 2:19 Jesus answered, "Destroy this sanctuary, and in three days
> I will raise it up!"

Three is the symbolic number of the Spirit. His answer means therefore: "Go on destroying this Temple with your superstition, this symbol of the vital impulse of every man; in three days— i.e., in conformity with the demands of the life of the spirit—I will renew, I will purify the soul of whoever wants to listen to me." The answer given to the Pharisees demanding a miracle is a direct answer to their question and insinuation. Each time a miracle is demanded or each time people claim to believe in him because of the so-called miracles, Jesus will give the same answer in different symbolic expressions. His contempt for the belief in miracles is stressed by the last verses of the passage; cures— mistaken for miracles—occur:

> 2:23 During his stay in Jerusalem for the Passover, many believed
> in his name when they saw the signs that he gave.
> Many believed because of the cures Jesus caused, of the fame

he started to have: they admired the man, but not the essence manifested through him.

2:24 but Jesus knew them all and did not trust himself to them,

2:25 he never needed evidence about any man, he could tell what a man had in him.

Thus, in the words of the Evangelist himself, Jesus does not trust all these people who surround him and the belief he arouses seems very suspicious to him. He therefore cannot cause cures whose purpose would be to make him appear as the Messiah because he knows only too well that the exalted hope directed toward him could easily be turned into disappointment if he cannot perform the "miracles" that the crowd demands.

It is important at this point to stress the real nature of these cures mistaken for miracles. They are, in fact, either symbolic cures, of which more later, or cures of symptoms of hysterical and psychosomatic illnesses, which still exist today.

Those called by myth "possessed by evil spirits"—i.e., nervous people, exalted in the spirit—often suffer from hysterical symptoms. Some paralyses have a purely psychic origin without any organic damage. Being a common phenomenon, hysterical paralysis is cured by the suggestive force of a more or less sublime belief. Hysterical paralysis is the expression of an exalted guilt in the face of overriding material and sexual desires that are themselves exalted. The patient, feeling overwhelmed by an irrepressible yearning to satisfy his exalted desires, "creates" a paralysis of psychic origin so as to get away from the impulsiveness of his desires.

Two forces are thus coexisting: the exalted desires attempting to break loose and the exaggerated guilt that opposes them. These two forces, being contradictory in their purpose, cancel one another; there remains only inhibition and its spectacular expression: paresis. The patient surrenders, as it were, to his guilt. But the latter being exalted—i.e., perverse—does not free the patient from his guilty desires; on the contrary, it strikes him with excessive punishment: the sick person is stuck in bed, incapable of moving. This is the punishment he imposes on himself for wanting to satisfy his exalted sexual and material appetites; this symptom is at the same time the expression of a very great vanity: the sick person cuts himself off totally from a world that is unworthy of him, he accuses the world, and is sentimentally given to self-pity since he cannot live like the others, as his great soul does not allow him to do so.

As soon as guilt can be freed from its exaltation, the inner convulsion gripping the psyche and expressing itself organically disappears, together with the symptoms.

At Lourdes as well as at Epidaurus in ancient Greece, such cures have been frequent. It is enough for a sick person having a sufficiently intense belief to believe himself (through auto-suggestion) forgiven by the divinity, to become free of the symptom. A psychological explanation of the phenomenon, together with a change in motivation, can obtain the same result. But a change of motivations has an advantage over autosuggestion: it is healthy for the psyche and modifies the whole makeup of the personality. A hysterical person as long as he remains hysterical can give up a symptom, but he will produce another one. On the other hand, if the psychic makeup is made healthy, the capacity to produce symptoms can definitively disappear. The suggestibility of these hysterical natures is certainly enhanced when it is faced with the personality of a man like Jesus. Jesus knew this all the more so that these times, still close to myth, knew far better than we do the relationship between psyche and soma. Organic disease was seen as the just punishment for a psychic disorder, which in a way is an insufficient conception, though on the other hand it is far deeper than our materialistic vision, which radically separates body from psyche. Today we see that even microbic diseases can be aggravated by a weakening of the individual's resistance due to inner disharmony.

Since every thought, every feeling of ours is more or less externalized through mimicry, tone of voice, harmony of the features or their convulsion, it is quite certain that Jesus—whose energy was to the highest degree converted into essential energy, superconscious concentration—had a unique radiance. This "divine" (symbolically speaking) radiance was particularly evident to men of great vital impulse such as John the Baptist and Peter but also to suggestible characters; their suffering moved Jesus, he endeavored to cure them by granting them his pardon—i.e., by freeing them of their guilt—but also by awakening their essential impulse and thus reducing their exalted attraction to the accidental. Would this not be the true significance one must give to the word "miracle"?

Yet Jesus does not like manifestations that might seem miraculous, that superstition might consider as supernatural. Jesus asks the sick people who have been suddenly cured not to speak of their cure. He loves to help, but he does not want to increase the misunderstanding of his mission and encourage superstition, feeling that the latter is closing in on him. Thus it is not out of fear of the Pharisees that he imposes silence on those who have been cured since his stance is almost offensive; without any fear, impelled by the nature of his true mission, he does not miss one single opportunity to attack the error he sees in the superstition of the old dogmatic belief.

However, his need to help is so great that he overcomes his aversion for public cures; he is even led to perform cures in front of crowds in spite of crowds, and in front of the Pharisees in spite of them. The force emanating from him becomes so powerful that "miracles" occur wherever he goes. And this, almost in spite of himself, for though he wants to help, he would rather save and awaken the souls than cure the bodies. How could he not be aware that suggestive belief, capable of curing the bodies, is not always living faith, which cures the soul and which he would like to inspire. Somewhat saddened and full of indulgence, he tells the cured people, "Go in peace, your faith has helped you." This indicates that he understands quite well that his spectacular cures, brought about by his love and feared by him because of his sublime prudence, are due to a quite natural influence and not to a supernatural force that he would attribute to himself. He also understands why this suggestive power leaves him when he goes to his native place where these very people, who could have been reached elsewhere, show themselves resistant and cannot take seriously the son of the carpenter they have known when he was a youth. Suggestive belief cannot be awakened:

Mt 13:57–58 A prophet is only despised in his own country and in his own house.

Is it necessary to add that a supernatural force would have been manifested in any place? The lack of importance given by Jesus to these external signs, the so-called miracles, is clearly expressed in the answer he gives to the Pharisees when they ask for a miracle:

Lk 12:39 It is an evil and unfaithful generation that asks for a sign.

What new sign could convince them, since the cures that have already been achieved did not convince them, and the manifold cures, instead of convincing them, will make them say,

Lk 11:16 It is through Beelzebub, the prince of devils, that he casts out devils.

Therefore it could not be in order to convince people that Jesus multiplies cures but to help, even when he cannot save. He clearly points out the difference, because when he is touched by the genuine humility of Mary Magdalene, he does not say, "Your faith has helped you" but

Lk 7:50 Your faith has saved you, go in peace.

Suggestive belief helps the body, but true faith saves the soul. The soul of the sinful woman is helped because all her carnal loves are forgiven her, thanks to her sublime love, thanks to her deep and true faith.

It happens also that Jesus himself glorifies what only a misunderstanding of symbolism calls "miracles"; for instance, when the disciples of John come to ask him whether he is the Messiah (see Mt 11:2–11, Lk 7:22–28): "Go back and tell John what you have seen and heard: the blind see again, the lame walk, the lepers are cleansed and the deaf hear, the dead are raised to life, the Good News is proclaimed to the poor and happy is the man who does not lose faith in me."

But these so-called "miracles" are precisely not cures of the body, but cures of the soul, which more than anything else witness to his mission (for instance, the cure of the man born blind). Such are not externally visible signs but internal and invisible signs, expressed by symbols. To the disciples of John, Jesus gives a symbolic answer in order to underline the true sense of his mission. The blind who see, the lame who walk, the lepers who are cleansed, the deaf who hear, the dead who are raised to life, are not those who are afflicted in their bodies but men who were blind and deaf to the truth and who—even though they are rare—did finally see it and hear it. They are the lame of the soul who straighten up and the dead of the soul who awaken. And because this is the case, Jesus can sum up his answer: "The Good News is proclaimed to the poor"—i.e., to those who are poor in essential life and receive the annunciation of the Good News— even in the midst of decadence, each and everyone of us can rise from death of the soul, find the essential anew. These symbolic "cures," no less frequent than the cures of symptoms or of hysterical illnesses, do not therefore contain any supernatural element. The supernatural aspect of the symbolic "miracles" stems from a confusion of reality with symbol.

Jesus himself objects many times to the superstition that, not understanding the meaning of his words and deeds, would see the "miracles" as proofs to shore up a false belief; he also opposes the other superstition, which in fact is the same, and would see in the prophecies of the Old Testament, the prediction of his personal life, historically accidental.

Dogmatism, misunderstanding—as the people wound up misunderstanding it—the meaning of the covenant and the meaning of the prophecies, taking symbols for facts, sought to prove that the prophecies miraculously foresaw the life of Jesus. By isolating passages of the Old Testament, dogmatism sought to erect a whole system of quotes predicting the life of the man Jesus from birth to death, stage by stage. It suffices to read the texts and to reinsert the isolated quotes in their context in order to realize that most of the quotes do not refer either to the humiliation of Jesus or to the triumph of his enemies, but to the humiliation of the Jewish people and to the triumph of its enemies. For these are not predictions but complaints about a specific situation (see Jer 7:11 or Ps 22:19, also page 211 of this work). The true predictions, also contained in the Old Testament, lose the supernatural aspect that is ascribed to them, if the confusion between Jesus and the Christ is avoided. They announce the messianic mission of Christ and not the historical life of Jesus.

The "Anointed" of the Lord is he who lives according to the truth and thus saves mankind from essential perdition. Thus, Christ, but not Jesus, was expected by the prophets who predicted its coming.

To affirm his messianic mission, Jesus quotes these prophecies, while objecting to the confusion. The central fact of such a confusion—making of the mythical hero, savior of mankind, a victorious king, savior of the Jewish people—is the misunderstanding of the symbol of the descent from David; precisely in order to oppose this central misunderstanding, Jesus says,

MK 12:35

> How can the scribes maintain that the Christ is the son of David?
> David himself, moved by the Holy Spirit, said:
>> "The Lord said to my Lord:
>> sit at my right hand
>> and I will put your enemies
>> under your feet."
> David himself calls him Lord, in what way then can he be his son?

If Christ is the Lord of David, he is not his son; Christ himself is seated "at the right hand of God," which clearly indicates the spiritual descent of the Messiah, symbolic son of God: therefore he is not the temporal descendant of David, his son, and he is not promised, like him, as the Pharisee and the people hope, an earthly success.

Analyzed according to their true mythical and hidden meaning whose translation is adequately founded on psychological phenomena and on the symbolism of all cultures, neither the prophecies nor the miracles therefore contain any supernatural element. Such an interpretation contradicts the mythical meaning of the prophecies as well as the mythical meaning of the Gospels. Wherever it is found in the Gospels, it can only be due to the misunderstanding of the Evangelists themselves or of later interpreters.

The whole of the second chapter, composed of incoherent elements, becomes, translated in such a way, a coherent illustration of the beginning of the mission and a significant summary of the mission's meaning. This coherence is only interrupted by two passages, which are clearly later interpolations. The interpolated passages are presented as explanatory supplements whose intention is evident; the second in particular contradicts the deep meaning of the Gospel. The first interpolation can be noted without comments, since it neither adds nor subtracts anything; it only testifies to a naive need to justify the mission, not by its deep and true meaning, but by passages from the Old

Testament. Thus, after the intervention in the Temple against the merchants, it is said,

2:17 Then his disciples remembered the words of scripture: "Zeal for your house will devour me."

It would have been superfluous even to mention this interpolation had it not been a prelude to another one that runs counter to the translation we gave for verses 13 to 15 of chapter 2. According to this second interpolation, the Temple is not the symbol of essential life but the body of Jesus. The Jews do not understand how he could raise up the Temple in three days; according to the interpolation,

2:21 But he was speaking of the sanctuary that was his body
2:22 and when Jesus rose from the dead, his disciples remembered that he had said this, and they believed the scripture and the words he had said.

The proposal of destroying his body has, at that point, no connection with the situation in which Jesus finds himself; such a meaning would destroy the coherence of the chapter: Jesus, contrary to his constant contempt for miracles (we will give additional proofs), contempt expressed by the end of the same chapter, proposed a miraculous happening to the Pharisees: the resurrection of his body; his disciples started—if we believe the passage—to believe quite late; unfortunately not because of the faith demanded by Jesus but because of a miracle. Such a naiveté is visibly an invitation to the disciples of the interpolator (more numerous than those of Jesus and constituting the rank and file of Christianity) to believe themselves in the miracle of miracles, the miraculous proof of the truth of the Scriptures, the resurrection of the body of Jesus.

CHAPTER 8

The Samaritan Woman; The Cure of the Official's Son

Chapter 3, the dialogue with Nicodemus, is the beginning of the symbolic teaching that runs throughout the entire Gospel. It will be analyzed later.

Chapter 4 interrupts the symbolic teaching with two illustrative episodes: the conversation with the Samaritan woman at the well and the cure of the son of a Roman official. The fact that these two episodes are linked in one chapter tends to indicate that they are based, in spite of an apparent difference, on a common theme. Such a common theme could only be the broadening of the mission, the indication that the mission is not only meant for the Jewish people but also for the Samaritans—whom the Jews detested—and for the pagans.

4:6 . . . it was about the sixth hour
4:7 when a Samaritan woman came to draw water, Jesus said to her: "Give me a drink."

The sixth hour is the hottest of the day. Jesus' request is not symbolic at all; it is enough to confront this verse with the following ones in order to be convinced.

4:9 "What? You are a Jew and you ask me, a Samaritan, for a drink?"—Jews in fact do not associate with Samaritans.

With such a request that cancels barriers, Jesus already provokes a gesture of surprise, alertness, amazement; by requesting something, he prepares the woman in turn to ask for something. Indeed, he tells her,

4:10 "If you only knew what God is offering and who it is that is saying to you: 'Give me a drink,' you would have been the one to ask, and he would have given you living water."

"If you knew the gift I have received from God, the strength of the vital impulse that is in me, if you knew who it is who is asking for a drink, you would have asked him to quench your inner thirst and he would have given you the essential truth." Thus here, the "living water" is contrasted to the real water. The Samaritan woman can actually give water to Jesus but only he can essentially quench her thirst.

4:14 "but anyone who drinks the water that I shall give will never be thirsty again: the water that I shall give will turn into a spring inside him, welling up to eternal life."

This spring is truth, the certainty that nothing is more important for man than to find inner harmony, the condition for which is to dare to see the truth about oneself. Only the truth can give the definitive solution to the problem of life, the feeling that, no matter what happens, nothing can destroy faith in the essence, faith in the meaning of life, the certainty that life has a meaning, that it is ruled by the organizing spirit. The water it will give, the truth received by the one who listens to it, will be the spring endlessly welling into spiritualization (understanding) and sublimation (love) leading him to essential life, to eternal truth.

4:16 "Go and call your husband," Jesus said to her, "and come back here."
4:17 The woman answered: "I have no husband."
4:18 He said to her: "You are right to say 'I have no husband' for although you have had five, the one you have now is not your husband. You spoke the truth there."

It is quite likely that the Samaritan woman of the Gospel was not married and was living together with a man. But that she would have had five husbands is really quite unlikely and that Jesus would have known it is totally unbelievable; the symbolic plane enables us to introduce the negative significance of the number 5,[34] which indicates convention; 5, in the decimal system, is dividing 10 into 2. It symbolizes, in its positive significance, the happy medium, harmony; in its negative significance, a pseudoharmony with the environment, a conventional attitude toward life. Which means that the Samaritan woman married the conventional spirit and that, because of this, the spirit now animating her (the man with whom she lives) cannot be considered as a "husband," a fecundating spirit; i.e., one that is capable of ensuring the essential direction of her life.

When she says later on,

4:29 "Come and see a man who has told me everything I ever did. I wonder if he is the Christ?"

one must understand, of course, "Here is a man who has taught me about all the mistakes I made."

4:21 Jesus said:
"Believe me woman, the hour is coming when you will worship the Father neither on this mountain nor in Jerusalem."

4:23 "But the hour will come—in fact it is here already—when true worshipers will worship the Father in spirit and truth; this is the kind of worshiper the Father wants."

The hour comes when the worship of God will not be done through rituals but according to the heart of man who will become the sanctuary in which dwells essential desire. For this to happen, men must be torn away from superstition and be shown essential truth, which can be grasped through the manifest world.

4:24 God is spirit and those who worship must worship in spirit and truth.

This verse is very important. "God is spirit" does not mean that God is a pure spirit floating in the air and freed from matter. The superconscious vision animating the Evangelist and enabling him to express himself symbolically is too profound for such an absurdity.

"God is spirit" means God is the symbol of the organizing spirit at work in the whole of nature. Its function is to organize matter and this must be understood for man to be able to worship in spirit (and not only according to the letter), in the truth of what it is. One must bow down to this mysterious organization to which man belongs, without crediting the cause to a real god, a dangerous idol.

The end of the chapter does not call for explanation. Only verses 37 and 38 deserve attention. They show that the Evangelists, careless as were all the ancients about historical truth, introduced into the narrative facts of their own time; this does not detract from the authenticity of the words of Jesus, but it shows that when the Gospel of John was written, at the end of the first century, the harvest of spirits sensitive to the message of Jesus was rich; the Evangelists had an audience.

> 4:37 For here the proverb holds good:
> one sows, another reaps.
> 4:38 I sent you to reap
> a harvest that you had not worked for.
> Others worked for it;
> and you have come into the reward of their trouble.

Those who worked are the prophets who came before Jesus, and above all, Jesus himself. The Evangelists, addressing themselves to spirits that are now open, reap the harvest of the spiritualization-sublimation of the Son of Man, his words, and his example.

Jesus leaves Judaea, and after crossing Samaria, he arrives in Galilee; he had understood (4:44) "[that] there is no respect for a prophet in his own country."

> 4:46 He went again to Cana in Galilee, where he had changed the water into wine. Now there was a court official there whose son was ill at Capernaum,
> 4:47 and hearing that Jesus had arrived in Galilee from Judaea, he went and asked him to come and cure his son as he was at the point of death.

Verse 46 shows that Jesus' fame is already established in Cana, where he had spoken and brought the essential message.

Jesus can no more really cure the dying man than he can change real water into real wine. But he can symbolically resurrect the dead of soul, the banalized, by bringing to them the shock of truth and thus tearing them away from the platitude of their life, restoring its intensity to their vital impulse.

The son mentioned in verse 47 is a symbolic image. A child is, for every human being, a hope, the hope of surviving oneself. Man is the symbol of the spirit. The son is therefore the hope of the spirit. This hope is threatened by death, by banalization. The official thus feels deeply disoriented with regard to the meaning of life. But he has heard what Jesus offers and would like to invest his vital impulse in it: however, his conviction is not strong enough, he needs an external sign.

> 4:48 Jesus said: "So you will not believe unless you see signs and portents!"

Which means, with respect to the motives of the official, "You come to me, because you have heard about me and what I said, yet you remain disoriented, threatened by banalization. For you to have faith in what I offer to you, you need a miracle." Faced by this unmasking of his false motives, the official is touched.

> 4:49 "Sir," answered the official, "come down before my child dies."

Which means, "Come down in me, talk to me, tear me away from banalization before my spirit dies. I am ready to hear you."

> 4:50 "Go home," said Jesus, "your son will live."

"If you want your spirit not to die, you have the vital impulse to understand it, it will not die." Such an affirmation would have no meaning if Jesus had not first spoken to the official, seeking and succeeding in awakening in him essential desire.

> 4:50 . . . the man believed what Jesus had said and started on his way.

The man had faith in the words that Jesus had spoken to him. Undoubtedly there were many words, though they are not recorded; the same words that would be developed later on in the teaching of Jesus. They enable the official to resume his way, his inner dynamics.

> 4:51 and while he was still on the journey back, his servants met him with the news that the boy was alive.

His servants—if we transpose them to the essential plane— are, in a positive context, the inner energies capable of satisfying him essentially. In a negative context, they would be the destructive energies (see the Introduction).

He is still at the stage of descending vanity, the confession of his vanity that had been forgetfulness of the essential, when his servants, his sublime forces (see Mt 4:11, ". . . angels appeared and looked after him") are already awakened and thus bring the news of the cure. Thanks to the sublime impulse being awakened in him, after having recognized the vanity of his past life, he feels that he is on his way to a cure, on his way to a renewed hope in life.

4:52 He asked them when the boy had begun to recover. "The fever left him yesterday," they said, "at the seventh hour."

Now the number 7 is, in all mythologies, the figure of the incarnation because it unites 4, the earth number, to 3, the spirit number.[35] Therefore he felt better at the hour when the words of Jesus started to become incarnate in him, to be emotionally understood.

4:53 The father realized that this was exactly the time when Jesus had said, "Your son will live," and he and all his household believed.

He was effectively cured at the moment when Jesus, having put his trust in his vital impulse, opened his spirit to his message without any sign or portent.

CHAPTER 9

The Paralyzed Man
at Bethzatha

In order to understand this chapter, we must go back to the explanations concerning the cures of symptoms or hysterical illnesses (cf. p. 84).

The Synoptic Gospels relate a cure that is altogether analogous and psychologically more understandable than the cure recorded by John, of which more later.

Luke narrates the "cure of the paralyzed man":

Lk 5:18 Then some men appeared, carrying on a bed a paralyzed man whom they were trying to bring in and lay down in front of him.

5:19 But as the crowd made it impossible to find a way of getting him in, they went up on to the flat roof and lowered him and his stretcher down through the tiles into the middle of the gathering, in front of Jesus.

5:20 Seeing their faith, he said: "My friend, your sins are forgiven you."

After the explanations about hysterical symptoms, the words of Jesus become quite clear. The paralytic man in the story is suffering above all from his "sins"; i.e., his material and sexual exaltations. Let us repeat that the vital error is not the satisfaction of natural desires, but their exaltation. Therefore, if Jesus "forgives" his sins, he thereby alleviates his convulsive and anxious guilty feelings and frees the sick man of his organic convulsion.

The certainty felt in his words, his tone, his physiognomy, his whole person, is certainly capable of being transmitted to this suggestible soul, to whom Jesus affirms that his sins are forgiven. This forgiveness will sooner or later bring about a physical cure, but since the Pharisees cry blasphemy:

Lk 5:21 The scribes and the Pharisees began to think this over. "Who is this man, talking blasphemy? Who can forgive sins but God alone?"

Jesus wants to show them that if he takes upon himself the right to "forgive" sins, it is because he has the real power to do so.

Lk 5:24 "But to prove to you that the Son of Man has authority on earth to forgive sins,"—he said to the paralyzed man—"I order you: Get up, and pick up your stretcher and go home."

This right to forgive sins is effectively sanctioned and justified by the fact that the paralyzed man "gets up, and picks up his stretcher and goes home"; cured of his guilty anxiety, he is freed of his hysterical symptom.

For the Pharisees, this is a conclusive proof:

Lk 5:26 They were all astounded and praised God and were filled with awe, saying: "We have seen strange things today."

Unfortunately this proof is swept away shortly thereafter by the petty arguments of vanity.

Lk 11:15 But some of them said: "It is through Beelzebub, the prince of devils, that he casts out devils."

This "cure" of the paralytic man in the Gospel of Luke stresses, as we have said, the direct connection between the cure and the forgiveness of sins, and thus the relationship between sins and sickness, "sin" being nothing but imaginative exaltation in all its forms.

In the Gospel of John, the symbolism being the same, we will not translate the details of the episode (6:16). This same connection between sin and sickness is established in two ways.

On the one hand, the word *Bethzatha* means "ditch." Even if it is the name of a district in north Jerusalem, it was certainly chosen for its meaning since the episode is symbolic. Now the "ditch" is the symbol of the subconscious, the unhealthy functioning of the psyche in the grip of imaginative exaltation. This paralyzed man of Bethzatha is thus clearly marked out as the hysterical sick person whose subconscious is heavily burdened.

On the other hand, when Jesus meets him again in the Temple, he calls him and tells him,

> Jn 5:14 "Now you are well again, be sure not to sin any more, or something worse may happen to you."

which means, "if you fall back into your sins, you run the risk of developing your symptoms again and even of going further, of overcoming guilty inhibition and becoming banalized; i.e., dying in the soul, which would be far worse."

The fault-punishment link is stressed again.

We shall not separate the "miracle of the multiplication of the loaves" from the teaching given about it. This is why this episode will be translated later in the part devoted to the symbolic teaching.

Verses 16 to 21 depict "the walk on the water." The episode, linked to the multiplication of the loaves, will be translated in the same chapter.

CHAPTER 10

The Reaction of the World

Chapter 7 clearly shows the reaction of the world to Jesus (7:1–13). Even his brothers are distrustful. The Jewish people are divided: some are for and others against him, without really knowing what to think: the high priests and Pharisees send their henchmen to make him stop: but his "time has not yet come" and the henchmen dare not seize him.

> Jn 7:6 Jesus answered: "The right time for me has not come yet, but any time is the right time for you."

The time when Jesus "will have conquered the world," as he will say later, has not yet come since the Son of Man has not yet completely freed himself from anxiety in the face of the world. That time will come. Then he will have overcome the seduction of the principle that rules the world, vanity; then will toll the bell for the hour of fulfillment; on the other hand, the time to banalize oneself is always here, ready to be achieved, for the brothers of Jesus and for all those who have no faith in essential life.

> 7:5 Not even his brothers, in fact, had faith in him.
> 7:7 "The world cannot hate you, but it does hate me, because I give evidence that its ways are evil."

Since the world hates me, when the hour of fulfillment will come, I will be eliminated by the world; you are not hated by the world because you subject yourself to it and to its principle, and essential life does not exist for you.

This passage therefore spells out the fatal danger threatening Jesus and that was already clearly announced as early as his first encounters with the Pharisees.

CHAPTER 11

The Woman Caught in Adultery

In the Law of Moses, stoning was the punishment for the crime of adultery (Jn 8:1–11). The stone being, in its negative significance, the symbol of banalization, stoning is the punishment to which the banalized being is subjected; he really dies under the hail of stones as he died in the soul under the assault of his desires of banalization.

The episode of the adulterous woman clearly shows that the Gospel is based on knowledge of the work of introspection.

In order not to be the first to cast a stone on the adulterous woman—i.e., to give oneself vainly the right to accuse her of banalization—one must, according to Jesus' advice, look into oneself. Who would not see there, if not the same faults, at least similar ones?

Elucidating introspection, objectivity about the self, is proposed by Jesus himself; it is simply the ability to place oneself face to face with one's vital shortcomings, not to project them as accusations onto others so as to exonerate oneself, not to fall into self-pity because of their consequences, not vainly to exalt the good intentions of being sublime that everyone wants to show as a proof of innocence; and, on the contrary, instead of repressing one's shortcomings with the help of false categorical justifications, to accept them in their human manifestations so as to dissolve them in the face of the clear dissatisfaction that they bring about.[36] The energy that is thus recovered can be invested in a psychic activity that is infinitely more efficacious than the ceaseless ruminations against the world and life. It can become the joy of feeling oneself freed from resentments, the joy of overcoming life's difficulties, the joy of feeling the good functioning of one's psyche, whose purpose is to achieve harmony.

This episode wonderfully illustrates one of the fundamental truths of the symbolic discourse: the sanctified man, the one who was sent, the son of the essence, has come to save and not to judge. Those who remain essentially dead are not condemned by him; they condemn themselves to dissatisfaction and loss of essential life. They will be condemned by the essence, harmony, the supreme law of life. They will not be judged by Jesus, the historical hero who is love and goodness; they will be judged by Christ: by the truth lived by Jesus, the eternal truth, the awareness everyone has of his own fault.

CHAPTER 12

The Cure of the Man Born Blind

Chapter 9 relates a most interesting episode: the cure of the man born blind. The miracle is entirely symbolic and must be translated in detail. The man born blind symbolizes the banal man, the man who since birth is blind to essential life. Confirmations of this significance are numerous, as we will see, throughout the narrative.

> 9:2 His disciples asked him: "Rabbi, who sinned, this man or his parents, for him to have been born blind?"
>
> 9:3 "Neither he nor his parents sinned," Jesus answered, "he was born blind so that the works of God might be displayed in him."

If the man was really blind, such an answer could have only one meaning: God made this poor man blind from birth so as to give himself the opportunity of a miracle. This is in fact the significance that is usually given to Jesus' reply.

In fact, it is unacceptable for Jesus to cure the blind man in order to convince people through a miracle; it would contradict the deep meaning of the entire Gospel and the condition for true faith that is often found in it (cf. the words of Jesus translated later in this book). The affirmation that, through the cure of a man born blind, the words of God become manifest must therefore have a symbolic meaning; and for them to have such a meaning, the man born blind must also have a symbolic significance. The man born blind symbolizes the man who is banal from birth. Neither he nor his parents have sinned, for banality, which must be distinguished from banalization, is not an individual fault but a biological one; it is, as it were, a weakness of nature itself against what could be called the spirit of life. The inadequacy inherent in the whole at appearance in all the forms of life subject to temporality, can be manifested in human nature through an impoverishment of essential life, a stagnation of the evolutionary impulse. During eras of decadence, banality, in conjunction with the banalization of current ideologies, leads to a generalized impoverishment.

Yet the spirit, the capacity for emotion in the face of the mystery of life is not absent in the banal individual and can be roused. But how difficult this is, and what strength of conviction must be expressed! Only the "Essence incarnate"—i.e., the human spirit at its highest level of spiritualization-sublimation such as the man Jesus achieved it—can, when it nourishes the essentially impoverished soul, accomplish this true "miracle"; yet it is not a portent. No other accomplishment will prove the power of essential desire, will manifest, like this one, the work of the spirit, symbolically called: the "works of God."

Since the man born blind symbolizes all banal men, thus banality itself, the unprecedented accomplishment of giving his sight to a man born blind, to the banal man, to awaken him to essential life, is the most powerful manifestation of the organizing spirit, of the divine in man. The words that Jesus adds confirm this significance:

> 9:4 "As long as the day lasts
> I must carry out the work of the one who sent me;
> the night will soon be here when no one can work.
> 9:5 "As long as I am in the world
> I am the light of the world."

If we were faced with a miracle-portent, these words would have no connection with the preceding ones. But explanation based on symbolism enables us to link all these verses. There is daylight as long as Jesus is in the world, the organizing spirit enlightens the world through him: this is the meaning of the sentence. After he has left the world, the night of banalization will rule again (since he could foresee that his message would not be truly understood, at least during the first centuries of Christianity). As long as he is in the world, he is the light of the world. Jesus is all the more inclined to call himself the "light of the world" that he is facing the man born blind, the soul living in the night of banality; nobody even thinks of mistaking this phrase "light of the world" for a fact.

It is vitally important that the "light of the world" enlighten the world; one can then understand the full depth of this phrase, which symbolizes the function of the man Jesus in the world of banalization. It is enough for the words of Jesus to touch this "blind man" for—symbolically—the eyes of the soul to open and for man to understand the importance of essential life. Therefore, to heal this blind man, the banal man, Jesus enlightens him with his word.

> 9:6 Having said this, he spat on the ground, made a paste with the spittle, put this over the eyes of the blind man
>
> 9:7 and said to him: "Go and wash in the Pool of Siloam" (a name that means "sent"). So the blind man went off and washed himself, and came away with his sight restored.

What takes place is not a real and magical manipulation, but a symbolic description of Jesus' behavior. Jesus "spits on the ground": to spit is an expression of contempt. "To lose one's saliva" means to speak with no efficacy. The saliva therefore symbolizes the words of Jesus but he does not speak in vain: his words express the low opinion he has of excessive attachment to earthly desires. With the help of his saliva, he makes mud out of the earth; thus, with the help of his word, his explanations, he shows the man the dirt of his exclusively earthly desires. He shows and demonstrates that exalted earthly desires are nothing but mud. He puts this mud on the closed eyes of the blind man; i.e., he exposes to his banal conscience the true significance of excessive earthly desires so as to "open his eyes," so as to make him understand that the exaltation of earthly desires is nothing but mud. He tells him,

9:7 "Go and wash in the Pool of Siloam" (a name that means "sent").

meaning, "Purify yourself from this banalization whose error you can see now, thanks to the work of spiritualization and sublimation that I represent; follow thus the example of the Messenger that I am, the sublime messenger of the 'essence.'"

> 9:7 So the blind man went off and washed himself and came away with his sight restored.

The banal man heeds the call and goes to purify his spirit; he needs a certain period of time to understand what Jesus has explained to him; he rises little by little to understanding. He will come back lucid and healed. Even banality can be cured by the power of the word of him who is sent. And in this cured blind man, in this purified banal man, the aspirations to the essential become real. Therefore the event is so astonishing that nobody wants to believe it.

9:8 His neighbors and people who earlier had seen him begging said: "Isn't this the man who used to sit and beg?"

The man "sitting on the ground," who found fulfillment in the platitude of exclusively earthly desires, who could not rise, elevate himself, this beggar content with what his impoverished life could offer him, begging from the outer world for the satisfactions that the world can give, incapable of giving himself essential satisfaction, how could he have been transformed, transfigured into a man "whose eyes are open," into a lucid man, into a purified and inspired being?

9:9 Others said: "No, he only looks like him." The man himself said: "I am the man."

And he relates how his eyes were opened. Therefore he tells what Jesus told him, what he explained to him: what words touched him, what meaning can be given to life (cf. 9:11).

Since the narrative of the former blind man concerns the essential and since people do not know where they can find Jesus, the man who has "opened his eyes," who has taught him what he himself is now capable of repeating, he is finally taken before the Pharisees (cf. 9:13).

The Pharisees, seeing a man of whom it is said that he never bothered with spiritual matters and who is suddenly speaking like an enlightened man, are astonished and want, in their turn, to know how the whole thing happened (cf. 9:15).

He repeats again what Jesus taught him, and shows that he has understood the substance. In the face of such an incredible transformation, the Pharisees themselves are split into two groups.

Since the transformation took place on a Sabbath, some say that a man who does not respect the Sabbath cannot be sent by

God. But others object that a sinner could not turn a banal man into an inspired one (cf. 9:16). Indeed, how could a sinner show a man who is blinded by error the joy of essential life, if he himself did not live it? Therefore they ask the now-seeing blind man what he thinks of this man who opened his eyes. He answers with all his faith, (9:17) ". . . he is a prophet." Then, the Pharisees, in order to find out if this man who is visibly inspired was really, from birth and until very recently, a banal man, have his parents brought before them (cf. 9:18). The parents assure them that he is their son, that he had no interest in essential life and that his eyes are now open; i.e., that he is sublimely transformed (cf. 9:20).

But they don't know the details; the Pharisees must talk to their son. "He is old enough, let him speak for himself." The parents are aware that it could be dangerous, in the presence of the Pharisees, to side too openly with their son and with the religious tenets that he voices (cf. 9:22).

The Pharisees call the man a second time and make him swear to tell the truth: how were his eyes opened? They want to know in detail the words of Jesus—a sinner in their eyes—who has yet accomplished that which they feel incapable of accomplishing (cf. 9:26).

Faced with the insistence of the Pharisees, the formerly "blind man" refers to what he has already said and expresses his surprise at the fact that the Pharisees want to know, in every detail, the words that were salutary to him.

9:27 He replied: "I have told you once and you would not listen. Why do you want to hear it all again? Do you want to become his disciples too?"

The Pharisees, hearing such an interpretation of their inquisitorial curiosity, get angry. How can one believe that this is their reason for being interested in what that man could have said?

9:28 At this they hurled abuse at him: "You can be his disciple," they said, "we are disciples of Moses."
9:29 "We know that God spoke to Moses, but as for this man, we don't know where he comes from."

Through the reference to Moses, to whom the superconscious impulse, symbolized by God, had spoken, the reply again expresses that the cure was wrought through words, but the latter—according to the Pharisees—are not from God. The cured banal man dares to defend his healer against the Pharisees.

9:30 The man replied: "Now, here is an astonishing thing! He has opened my eyes, and you don't know where he comes from?"

9:31 "We know that God does not listen to sinners, but God does listen to men who are devout and do his will.

9:32 "Ever since the world began it is unheard of for anyone to open the eyes of a man who was born blind.

9:33 "If this man were not from God, he couldn't do a thing."

The Pharisees, furious and shaken at the same time by the obviousness of these words, do not even dare to punish the unheard-of audacity of this awakened man.

9:34 "Are you trying to teach us," they replied. "And you a sinner through and through, since you were born!" And they drove him away.

Every sentence of this interrogation is significant for the authentic meaning of this episode, but the Pharisees' last exclamation is meaningful to the highest degree. For them the man born blind "was born in sin." For the Pharisees, the pure man, the man without sin, the opposite of the man born blind, is one who knows the Scriptures and believes according to the letter. For them, one who does not know the Scriptures word for word does not live spiritually. He is blind, while they are lucid.

9:35 Jesus heard that they had driven him away, and when he found him, he said to him: "Do you believe in the Son of Man?"

9:36 "Sir," the man replied, "tell me who he is so that I may believe in him."

9:37 Jesus said: "You are looking at him; he is speaking to you."

9:38 The man said: "Lord, I believe," and worshiped him.

The phrasing is not even "Do you believe in the son of God?" but "Do you believe in the Son of Man?" (though it is true that certain translations use the phrase "Do you believe in the Son of God?"). If the man born blind finds faith in the essential, it is clearly because a man showed to him that essential satisfactions are a greater promise of joy than accidental satisfactions. Thus, he can have faith in the hope contained in human life, and therefore also in himself; even if he is not the "Son of Man" in the unique way of Jesus, at least he can share in the greatness of life by also accepting the human condition in all its fullness.

In fact, there has been no miracle; the Son of Man acted only through his stance and through his words; the man born blind does not even know who the man was who cured him; the fame of Jesus, his visible authority, could not have acted to increase the convincing force of his words. It is only now, at the end of the narrative, that Jesus identifies himself. It is through his awakened and enthusiastic soul that this banal man has become capable of worshiping him who, apparently, is no different from any other man; he has seen the essential in this unique man, he has had faith in the Essence he manifests; he has seen what is invisible for many men who believe themselves to be lucid. This is conveyed by Jesus' reaction to the worship of the healed man:

> 9:39 Jesus said: "It is for judgment that I have come into the world
>   so that those without sight may see
>   and those with sight turn blind."

Again, he is not the judge; men judge themselves through their stance toward him. This judgment is rendered by their spiritual openness or banal narrowness. Those who are blind but do not claim to see are capable of being reached by the teaching of Jesus, and they will see, they will understand the truth. Those who claim to see and believe that they have a right vision are incapable of seeing anything. If there were still the slightest doubt, it is clear that these words, summing up the meaning of the narrative by contrasting those who have not seen and end up seeing, symbolized by the man born blind, and those who think they see and do not see, symbolized by the Pharisees, refer not to physical blindness and sight but to spiritual blindness and clearsightedness. This ending of the chapter contrasts the true faith of the man born blind, the cured banal man, to the false belief of the Pharisees, those who claim to see. Thus the symbolic narrative deals with this blindness and this clearsightedness. This symbolic meaning is stressed even further and brought back to the affirmation at the beginning of the narrative by its conclusion.

Some Pharisees who have heard the words of Jesus about the judgment of the blind who end up seeing and the seeing who are blinding themselves, ask him,

> 9:40 "We are not blind, surely?"

This is proof that they suspect it to be so.

This simple question confirms the translation we have given, because if the narrative dealt with organic sight, the Pharisees would not need to ask Jesus for an answer.

> 9:40 Jesus replied:
> "Blind? If you were,
> you would not be guilty,
> but since you say: 'we see,'
> your guilt remains."

It is thus obvious that the sin has the significance introduced at the beginning: "It is a sin against the spirit, the only one that will not be forgiven" (cf. Mt 12:32, Lk 12:10, Mk 3:28–30), blindness to the essential, justified and mistaken for the meaning of life. The man born blind, the banal man, has not sinned against the spirit of life; his spiritual blindness is caused by an incapacity and not by vain pretension. If the Pharisees were born blind, simple banal men, they would be without sin. But they believe themselves to be lucid, they are vain of their pseudoclearsightedness; they have blinded themselves with their pretension. Their sin remains; their fault is individual. They are individually responsible before the spirit of life, before the Essence.

Banality turned vain mistakes itself for the spirit; this conventional banalization, represented by the Pharisees in the Gospel, is the most dangerous enemy of all men and also of the Son of Man. It is the definitive death of the soul: in the grip of conventional banalization, convention of the spirit, deliberation is totally subjected to vanity and essential desire is totally stifled by this pretension regarding life. In the case of the wholly sanctified man, who has become fully Essence, this essential danger, this danger of death for the soul, no longer exists. Although it does remain as an outer danger, a lethal threat: the purified man is under attack from banalized people; the less the inner danger, the greater the outer danger. Banalized men, vain about their banalization, essentially dead souls, will not stand the living manifestation of the Essence, the sanctification of the unique man. They will make him die in his body. But this bodily death, this visible failure, will be the opportunity for the most decisive victory of inner life, essential life, victory of the Essence over the appearance. The dead souls will object to the victory of essential truth, they will take hold of it, will transform it into error and dead belief, in order to crush it; the struggle for essential truth will remain the essential meaning of mankind's history throughout the centuries, and again and again, the strength of the human vital impulse will overcome its most dangerous enemy, banalization of spirit, symbolized by the Pharisees (who are present at all times). The mythical vision of this victory, which is not a reality but an evolutionary promise, is evoked here to give its true meaning to the high points of all the Gospels, the symbolic Passion and Resurrection.

CHAPTER 13

The Resurrection of Lazarus

It cannot be stressed enough that in Scripture—just as in all myths—the subject is not the sickness and death of the body, but the sickness and death of the soul. In the Scriptures, death, since the myth of Genesis, where it appeared as the consequence of the fall of Adam, has this meaning, and it keeps it throughout all the mythical narratives, including the Gospels.

If the resurrection of Lazarus dealt with an actual event, it would have been—among all miracles—the most irresistibly convincing: resurrection of a man dead for four days, already decomposing and who, at the call of Jesus and in spite of his bound feet, leaves his tomb to go on living!

The resurrection of Lazarus is symbolic; it is victory over essential death. Lazarus is Jesus' friend, the man of strong vital impulse who has become prey to material and sexual banalization.

The tomb in which Lazarus is put symbolizes the punishment meted out: being shut up in the earth, a consequence of banalization. The myth, which is the expression of superconscious lucidity, always clearly shows the relationship between fault and punishment. The punishment is only an aspect of the vital error. He who has desired the exclusive satisfaction of earthly desires punishes himself. He limits himself to such pleasures, which have been perverted by exaltation; the myth shows, in a single image, "the tomb where he lies," his egocentric withdrawal, his "sin," and the punishment of this sin, the death of his essential impulse, of his interest for the essential, symbolized by real death.

The former friend of Jesus, who by this very fact is more prone to guilty feelings than any other man, plunged obstinately into a scandalous life, in order to drown out his torment, to stifle the inner voice. Jesus, knowing full well how this soul is undergoing an unbearable torture, calls him, and the call of his sublime friend, his former spiritual master, overcomes all this convulsed defiance, and all his resistance. It might be that the crowd that was present saw such a sudden conversion, such irresistible influence, as a miracle. Here is the verse-by-verse translation:

11:3 The [two] sisters sent this message to Jesus: "Lord, the man you love is ill."

This concerns, as we have already said, the illness of the soul.

11:4 On receiving the message, Jesus said: "The sickness will end not in death but in God's glory, and through it the Son of God will be glorified."

This explanation by Jesus is altogether the same as the one he had given in the case of the man born blind (9:3): "This sickness will end not in death, not in the definitive banalization of Lazarus, but in God's glory, in the victory of the essential over the accidental, for my word is capable of tearing away from the seduction of pleasures the soul that has sunk in them."

Jesus decides to go to Lazarus, but the disciples are surprised that he wants to go back to Judaea where the Jews attempted to stone him.

11:6 Yet when he heard that Lazarus was ill he stayed where he was for two more days
11:7 before saying to the disciples: "Let us go to Judaea."
11:8 The disciples said: "Rabbi, it is not long since the Jews wanted to stone you; are you going back again?"
11:9 Jesus replied:
"Are there not twelve hours to the day?
A man can walk in the daytime without stumbling
because he has the light of the world to see by.
11:10 "But if he walks at night he stumbles, because there is no light to guide him."

"To each day the evil thereof is sufficient," he tells them; "as long as I accomplish my mission, what happens is not important. The only thing to be avoided is to walk in the dark."

11:11 He said that and then added: "Our friend Lazarus is resting. I am going to wake him."

Lazarus enjoys the false rest of the spirit, the banalizing sleep, but my words will wake him up.

11:12 The disciples said to him: "Lord, if he is able to rest, he is sure to get better."

This shows that the disciples themselves have misunderstood the words of Jesus. Were Lazarus somatically ill, a rest would indeed be the way to recovery.

11:13 The phrase Jesus used referred to the death of Lazarus, but they thought that by "rest" he meant "sleep."

The verb "to rest" is used in the meaning of dying in the soul, as the text spells it out: this is a complete sleep of the spirit, expressing the death of the soul.

11:14 so Jesus put it plainly: "Lazarus is dead
11:15 "and for your sake I am glad that I was not there because now you will believe. But let us go to him."

Lazarus has given himself over to banalization, and in a way I am glad that he went all the way in his error. Since Lazarus has tasted these perverse satisfactions, you will not be able to say when he comes back to essential life, that he subjected himself in a moralizing way to the truth. No one can leave the satisfactions of banalization unless he replaces them with the more intense satisfactions of the essential. There you will see that the truth I offer him is more satisfying than error. And you will have faith in the essential.

11:16 Then Thomas—known as the Twin—said to the other disciples: "Let us go too, and die with him."

"We too are banalized people, but one can be reborn from banalization. Let us go and listen to what he will say and we will die to sin." We see here, the dual meaning of the verb "to die," which is constantly found in the Epistles of the apostle Paul (see the translation of the Epistles [37]): either to die to sin; i.e., "to be resurrected," to be reborn to essential life; or to die through sin; i.e., to become banalized. Thomas, being a disciple of Jesus, cannot want to become banalized, otherwise why would he follow Jesus? But he desires very deeply to be freed from the temptation

Jesus? But he desires very deeply to be freed from the temptation of banalization, to die to sin.

11:17 On arriving Jesus found that Lazarus had been in the tomb for four days.

Four is the number of earthly desires; in its negative significance, it symbolizes the exaltation of earthly desires, banalization. The symbol of the tomb was translated at the beginning of this chapter. If Lazarus has been in the tomb for four days, it means that he has sunk into banalization. He is now dead in the soul.

11:21 Martha said to Jesus: "If you had been here, my brother would not have died."

You were the friend of my brother. My brother had a great impulse toward the essential, otherwise you would not have befriended him and he himself would not have been interested in your teaching. Had you been here, your words would have torn him away from temptation. And now, I fear that you cannot pull him out of his banalization. To which Jesus replies:

11:23 "Your brother will rise again!"

Jesus could not make such a statement if he did not trust Lazarus, whom he had known very well. Yet Martha is troubled by doubts: is it possible to tear oneself away from such banalization?

11:24 Martha said: "I know he will rise again at the resurrection on the last day."

When he dies in the body, he will return to the unfathomable mystery whence he came. This alludes to the metaphysical resurrection, of which more will be said when we deal with the teaching of Jesus. It remains an image, because all that deals with what lies "beyond" this spatiotemporal world is not accessible to understanding. But Jesus is talking about a possible moral resurrection, taking place during life. And thus,

11:25 Jesus said:
"I am the Resurrection [and the Life]."

I bring the resurrection; that is, the possibility of an inner renewal, I bring essential life, and you cannot doubt this.

11:26 ". . . If anyone believes in me, even though he dies,
he will live.
And whoever lives and believes in me
will never die.
Do you believe this?"

How could such words apply to actual death? Would Jesus
have lied? For it is obvious that many believed in him, and many
do so today, and yet they die. On the other hand, it is not incredible to believe that man, even though he sinks into banalization,
death of the soul, will recover the life of the soul if he rediscovers
faith in the essential. As to one who does not cease to have faith
in the essential, he does not run the risk of falling into banalization. Martha replies:

11:27 "Yes, Lord, I believe that you are the Christ, the Son of God,
the one who was to come into this world."

Thus does Martha witness to her faith in the truth embodied
by the man Jesus, he is the Christ, the anointed of the Lord, the
symbolic Son of God, he who was always announced by the wise
foresight of the superconscious, because in this people that gave
so many prophets, in this people that had so many men of strong
vital impulse rising again and again against banalization, it was
credible—not to say certain—that a man carrying eternal truth,
symbolized by the Almighty, would incarnate it to the extent of
sanctity.

11:31 When the Jews who were in the house sympathizing with Mary
saw her get up so quickly and go out, they followed her, thinking
that she was going to the tomb to weep there.

The Jews, friends of the two sisters, were there to sympathize
with them, and probably also to enjoy to a certain degree the
misdeeds of their brother, a feeling that could be insidiously
manifested against Jesus, for what was the point of having Jesus
for a friend, of having been taught by him, if it ended up with
such a piteous fall into debauchery? They suppose that Mary, in
her haste to go out, is again going to weep thinking about her
brother's follies. To go to the tomb is to evoke in imagination the
loss of essential life and the punishment (pain) stemming from
it.

11:32 . . . "Lord, if you had been here, my brother would not have
died!"

11:33 At the sight of her tears, and those of the Jews who followed
her Jesus said in great distress with a sigh that came straight
from the heart . . ."

Jesus is angry at the error of banalization. He is not angry at
Lazarus since, as he said many times, he did not come to judge
but to save, which shows his full understanding of human weakness. Yet his joy is troubled by the perverse deviation of his
friend.

11:34 "Where have you put him?" They said:
"Lord, come and see."

Come and see with your own eyes where he is, how low he
has stooped in banalization. Undoubtedly they explain to Jesus
the debauchery into which Lazarus sank, his bad habits, wine,
women, sloth, gambling, the wrong life.

11:35 Jesus wept.
11:36 and the Jews said: "See how much he loved him!"

Now the saint is freed from any affective attachment. He cannot weep for the bodily death of a friend, even a beloved one.
That would be a sign of incomprehensible weakness. What links
the saint to another man cannot be sentimental tenderness; it can
only be the hope of seeing his message accepted by a being
whose vital impulse is more intense than that of many other
men.

In the house where, more than in any other, Jesus has been
generously welcomed, even when he was already threatened,
such a soul could be found. This being, representing all mankind, has awakened in Jesus the sublime hope of being heard.
The bodily death even of such a friend would only be something
due to nature, to be calmly accepted. Only the moral defeat of a
deeply loved being can, for a moment, trouble a saintly soul
because the possibility of this defeat would mean the possibility
of defeat for all mankind; it does for a moment trouble the spirit
of Jesus, his love for the world and the sublime hope he puts in
his mission.

11:37 But there were some who remarked: "He opened the eyes of the
blind man, could he not have prevented this man's death?"

Some use the banalization of Lazarus to cast doubt on the truth brought by Jesus, the meaning of his mission, by saying: since—according to what people say—his word enabled one man who was completely derived of essential life, to open up to the truth, could he not have convinced Lazarus and prevented him from ever falling into banalization?

The answer to this objection is the weakness of human nature. It is precisely because the influence of Jesus is not miraculous at all that it can also be lost. Lazarus, like Jesus, remains bound by the laws of psychic functioning. The former friend of Jesus, having little by little forgotten the teaching he had received, let himself be caught into banalization: but, necessarily more a prey to guilty feelings than others because his vital impulse is stronger, he sank into a life of debauchery so as to stifle the inner voice more strongly.

> 11:38 Still sighing, Jesus reached the tomb: it was a cave with a stone to close the opening . . .

The cave, like any obscure or underground thing, is a symbol of the subconscious. The stone, either seen as something solid (Simon became "Peter, the Rock" because his faith is as strong as a rock) or on the contrary is viewed as something sterile, will then be a positive or negative symbol. Here, associated with the darkness of the subconscious (the cave), it is a symbol of banalization; the phrase "heart of stone" is very eloquent. Jesus thus finds himself before the tomb of Lazarus, before Lazarus himself whose body is the tomb of his dead soul. He is even face to face with the subconscious (cave) of Lazarus; all the petty arguments of banalization, the false valuations of banalization, the stone, close the opening of his psyche, his receptivity.

> 11:39 Jesus said: "Take the stone away."

To penetrate this psyche, which is thus invaded, one must first attack the banalizing justifications (take the stone away). Only the strength of Jesus' conviction is capable of opening a spirit beclouded by error.

> 11:39 . . . Martha said to him: "Lord, by now he will smell, this is the fourth day."

Now 4, as we have seen, is the negative symbol of the exaltation of earthly desires. Thus does Martha manifest her doubt with respect to Jesus' intervention. Lazarus is too deeply sunk in banalization, he cannot be recovered, his soul is already decomposed, disharmonized by the number 4, by material and sexual excess.

> 11:40 Jesus replied: "Have I not told you that if you believe you will see the glory of God?"

Jesus does not doubt for a moment his ability to tear Lazarus away from his life of debauchery. This "resurrection," this rebirth to the truth that had been momentarily forgotten by Lazarus, will show that essential satisfaction can be stronger than perverse satisfactions. This will be "the glory of God"; "the eternal truth" will become obvious. In these words addressed to Martha, Jesus goes even farther: "For you also, it is a matter of understanding," he tells her, "that essential satisfaction is above all other satisfactions; at this moment, I am not referring to him but to you. You doubt that I can, with my words, bring him back to essential life, but if you have faith, you will discover the importance of the essential, and you will see that I am right."

> 11:41 So they took away the stone. Then Jesus lifted up his eyes and said "Father, I thank you for hearing my prayer."

Note that Jesus speaks about a past action. God heard his prayer. Now the "miracle"—if there was a miracle—has not yet occurred. But if one remains on the symbolic plane, everything becomes clear: the stone that has been taken away (symbolizing the petty arguments of the attacked and eliminated banalization) has enabled the teaching of Jesus, the right valuations, to penetrate the psyche of Lazarus; the "miracle" has taken place: Lazarus has returned to the truth. Only the word of Jesus has been able to accomplish this conversion.

> 11:42 "I knew indeed that you always hear me
> but I speak
> for the sake of all these who stand around me
> so that they may believe that it was you who sent me."

I am always heard because I know that the essential is more satisfying than the accidental. I can always reestablish in myself the joy of harmony, I know the solution to all the problems I can pose myself. But I spoke for all these, to show that resurrection from the death of the soul is possible for a man of faith. Jesus stresses, "I speak for the sake of all these," which confirms that indeed he spoke to accomplish this "miracle." Now his words are not recorded and we must suppose what he said. What could he have said except words arousing in Lazarus a feeling of guiltiness in the face of his life's errors, regret for lost joy, and a call to nobler satisfactions? What he said to him is what he has already said many times, through the words recorded by the Evangelist, and we will translate them later on.

> 11:43 The dead man came out, his feet and hands bound with bands of stuff and a cloth around his face. Jesus said to them: "Unbind him, let him go free."

Lazarus, who was dead in the soul, frees himself from the false and banalizing justifications in which his spirit was mired. His activity (hands) and soul (feet; cf. the Introduction) still bear the mark of the bonds that tied him, on the one hand the bad habits he had fallen into, and on the other his erroneous valuations. His face—i.e., his way of facing life in this banalizing perspective—is still veiled by subconscious justifications (cloth around his face).

Yet, the "miracle" is already accomplished, Jesus has given thanks for it (11:41). But the stigmata of error are still visible on Lazarus, which is psychologically unavoidable.

Note that Jesus addresses himself to the onlookers "Unbind him, let him go free." Thus he asks them too to free him from his reputation of a banalized man, to give him another chance.

In the Gospel of John, where all is symbolism, the myth of Lazarus, placed before the outer defeat of the hero, before the humiliation of the Passion that the world inflicted on him, symbolizes the victory of his mission, in spite of the outer defeat that will ensue. The myth of Lazarus symbolizes the possible resurrection of mankind. The Passion, in spite of the outer defeat, is at the same time an inner victory that is not symbolic, but real, of the hero over the world and over all the suffering that the world can inflict.

As a whole, the illustrative scenes therefore show, more or less symbolically, the beginning of the mission, whose meaning is the struggle against the "death of the soul"; they show the inner victory over all the forms of essential death: banality, material and sexual banalization, and banalization of the spirit or cynicism; they also show the outer and lethal danger threatening the hero in this struggle, the apparent and outer defeat of the victorious hero. Since the struggle against essential death, against the perdition of the soul-Essence, is also the symbolic meaning of the teaching that obtains in the entire Gospel, these episodes that interrupt and finally crown this teaching are therefore an illustrative paraphrase of the words of Jesus.

Part 3

THE TEACHING OF JESUS

CHAPTER 14

General Significance

We wish to stress once more that the teaching placed by the Evangelist in the mouth of the hero may not even include one word of what Jesus actually said. Yet it reproduces faithfully what Jesus wanted to signify. This discourse is thus mythically true. It is in accordance with the most ancient mythical truth and is simply a detailed explanation—though it remains symbolic— of the myth created by Jesus himself and summed up in the phrase "Son of God." It expresses in a symbolic form the images of God, the Son, their relationship and the relationship of the "Son" with the world. The teaching contains in a symbolic condensation all the truth that the words and deeds of Jesus, his entire life, were able to express. The Gospel of John thus relates indirectly the tale of the historical hero, Jesus. *The real hero of the Gospel is the mythical hero, Christ.* The only purpose in using the real name, the name of Jesus, in the symbolic narrative is to symbolize the unity between Jesus and Christ.

In order to understand the meaning of the words of Jesus, it is sufficient to introduce the symbolic meaning of the Father: the mysterious Essence, the mysterious intentionality that can be perceived throughout the whole of nature, the creative harmony; it is manifested through the entire appearance by the fact of the harmonious organization of all existing phenomena. The awareness of this organization compels man to say that a spirit—defined as an organizing capacity—underlies all vital and prevital phenomena. But its manifestation does not prevent it from remaining mysterious in its cause, which will never be known to the human mind; it is an unfathomable mystery. The human spirit itself is but a special instance of this preconscious spirit, this organizing capacity that is at work in all that is. Being a tool in the search for satisfaction, it is an evolutionary modality.

The word *Father* is rooted in emotion. Man feels this mysterious demand for harmony animating him as if it were the demand of a "father" capable of guiding him through the dangers of life. In every person, the superconscious—an evolved form of instinct—takes on this function of essential guide, it is the "mythical father," frequently encountered in dreams.

"Son" must be understood as creative harmony that has become manifest, incarnate in the unique man, personification of truth and goodness.

"Death" must be understood in its symbolic significance, the loss of essential desire, of the animating vital impulse, of the soul-Essence; this essential death is manifested by an exclusive love for the accidental world.

Essential or "eternal" life must be understood as being animation through the truth-seeking spirit, enthusiasm in the quest for the essential, harmonization, and therefore also the capacity to understand the perfect manifestation of the creative harmony; i.e., the unique man.

When it comes to "resurrection," we have to introduce the awakening from the death of the impulse to essential life; such an awakening is effected with the help of the example of the life (essentially perfect) of the unique man, insofar as there is in the seeker of truth, the capacity to see and understand that Jesus is the manifestation of the "Essence," thus insofar as there is a genuine faith. Enthusiasm in the face of the achievement of this man, awakens in others the essential desire: this impulse of harmonization vivifies the soul anew, "resuscitates" it (see the resurrection of Lazarus). Only a life centered around the development of the vital impulse can bring definitive satisfaction, joy; only the satisfaction of essential desire can calm the dissatisfaction that is inherent in all lives. To refuse essential life because of the seduction of the world and anxiety in the face of the world, therefore means at the same time essential punishment; no judgment is added to this.

All the obscurity of Jesus' words vanishes if one introduces these constant significances, valid for the temporal life of the man Jesus; but also valid for the symbolic image of the Father-Essence and the soul-Essence, images that are suggestive and veracious *as long as one does not mistake them for realities existing outside of reality*, as long as one gives to the image its emotional significance of mystery.

Such obscurity also seems to disappear if one eliminates the mysterious depth from these words, if one completely does away with the feeling of mystery expressed by the God and soul symbols, if one mistakes the illogical symbolism of Jesus' words for a logical explanation, for a complete and actual revelation of "the mystery." No obscurity seems to remain if one understands the discourse literally and if one simply believes what is said, even if it is beyond belief, with the excuse that it is all the more profound that it cannot be proven. But it is not enough to decree that it be so in order for it to be so. What is unbelievable cannot awaken genuine faith and inevitably one is driven to speculate, to seek explanations that could mask unbelievable things, too easily accepted from the outset and not to be shaken off in spite of all explanations. Late and speculative explanations will only serve to turn what is unbelievable into absurdity. People will finally be compelled to bring themselves to believe not only in what is unbelievable but also in absurdity: *Credo quia absurdum.* But absurdity kills the spirit, and no other possibility will be left than to believe in order to believe, without thinking or feeling. This is dead belief. What disappears through literal understanding, through belief in the unbelievable, is not the obscurity but the feeling of mystery that is the condition for any true faith. The obscurity remains, it is only replaced by another form of darkness, by miracles, which are another expression of what is unbelievable. What this brings about is not true faith, called for by the texts themselves, but belief in miracles and portents. Instead of becoming aware of mystery, not the entity-mystery, but mystery for the human spirit—i.e., beyond the grasp of the human spirit—one is offered an actual God situated in the beyond; from there God comes down in order to impose himself through portents, but such a justification of miracles is only juggling. This is the direct opposite of the hidden and genuine meaning. This is a refusal to think, the death of the spirit, the consequence of the spirit accepting unbelievable things; the real God, an anthropomorphic ghost, is but an expression of the vain pretension of the accidental "ego," an exalted love of self, the senseless desire not to see this adored "ego" disappear and to find in an actual God someone who is capable of understanding its greatness, capable of rewarding it according to its just deserts. Such a pretension, disguised as love of God, is projected onto a beyond that is itself nothing more than a projection of this world. This is the greatest vanity that can be, it is vanity in the broadest meaning of the term, since nobody answers this call except an exalted imagination that can go as far as mystical delusion.

Dependence on the opinion of a real god becomes a constant motive of one's activity. A guilty worry that is purely imaginative and can turn into anxiety replaces essential guiltiness, or rather combines with it, depriving it of most of its evolutionary efficacy. The true fault is repressed; the imaginary fault—dealing with the relationships of human beings with this real God—is cultivated. Accusation of the others, repressed through pseudogoodness, imitating the real Son of the real God, springs out again from the subconscious, in the guise of a sentimental love and a dogmatism of sentiments. Thought is compelled to hang on to belief and to become rigid in a pseudocertainty. This misuse of the spirit leads the believer to doubt the reflective function, hallmark of the thinking being. All this is simply an exalted love of the appearance,* the direct opposite of the sublime love of the mysterious "Essence."

---

*See note on page 5. —Translator.

CHAPTER 15

The Conversation with Nicodemus

Just as the mission begins in a close circle, that of the Wedding at Cana, so the first discourse does not address itself to the world, but to one man, Nicodemus, though he is—because of his blindness—the representative of the enemy to be defeated, the Pharisees. Nicodemus comes to visit Jesus by night (3:1), which shows that he is hiding from his peers, being afraid to show his interest in the message of Jesus. However, he comes to Jesus in order to affirm that he believes in him:

> 3:1 There was one of the Pharisees called Nicodemus, a leading
> 3:2 Jew who came to Jesus by night and said: "Rabbi, we know that you are a teacher who comes from God for no one could perform the signs that you do unless God were with him."

The "miracles," be they symbolic (Lazarus) or in the guise of spectacular cures of hysterical and psychosomatic illnesses, will be, throughout the entire Gospel, one of the reasons for the crowds (6:14, 7:31, 10:21, 11:45) and for some Pharisees (12:42) to think that Jesus is a man of God. But this remains a very unsatisfactory motive because such a belief supposes a reference either to other people or to external facts. This is not real understanding of his message.

> 3:3 Jesus answered:
> "I tell you most solemnly
> unless a man be born from above
> he cannot see the kingdom of God."

You talk about God, but do you know who he really is? Are you born to the life of the spirit? Are you born from above?

The kingdom of God is inner life understood in its essential and mysterious dimension; to be able to take on oneself such a dimension of life is to develop true faith within the self. One must therefore be born again, wake up from the Pharisaic banalization and live in the essential. From the outset of Jesus' teaching, faith in the essential dimension of life is contrasted with the false belief of Nicodemus, the belief in miracles. From the outset of his public life, the condition for the understanding of Jesus' word is formulated.

3:4 Nicodemus said: "How can a grown man be born? Can he go back into his mother's womb and be born again?"

3:5 Jesus replied: "I tell you most solemnly, unless a man is born through water and the Spirit he cannot enter the kingdom of God."

With this question, Nicodemus shows that he is not even thinking about a life after death. Jesus replies that one must be reborn in the spirit. This rebirth in the spirit is linked to the purification of exalted desires, water being an allusion to baptism (see Chapter 1). Purification from the exaltation of the desires, essential life, "kingdom of God" have one and the same significance. Since to be reborn, to have eternal life and to resurrect are, throughout the entire Gospel, synonymous terms, it is already clear in this single passage that resurrection is resurrection, during life, of the spirit previously blinded by beliefs, and not resurrection of the body.

All the more so as Jesus adds,

> 3:6 "What is born of the flesh is flesh,
> what is born of the Spirit is spirit."

This is a clear invitation not to confuse carnal desires and essential, spiritual desire. A new birth can only be a rebirth of the spirit, which can only be an awakening of the spirit; this passage deals therefore with moral resurrection, inner revival, awakening from the banalization that holds Nicodemus in its grip. Jesus himself—or if you wish: the Evangelist—makes an important distinction between moral and metaphysical resurrection (further on, Jesus will say [3:12] that so far he has only spoken about "things in this world"; in others' words, resurrection during life, moral resurrection).

Here we must stress the distinction between moral resurrection and metaphysical resurrection. Moral resurrection is an awakening of the vital impulse, a return to the essential after the sloth of banalization. It is achieved during life. Banalization being called the death of the soul, or also the death of the animating impulse, a return to essential life can be called a *resurrection* since the Latin word that is at the root of the latter term means nothing else than "rise again."

On the other hand, metaphysical resurrection does not correspond to any reality of the spatiotemporal world. It is only an image. Since life did not emerge from absolute nothingness—out of which nothing can come out, as it contains nothing—it cannot return to nothingness; but where did it come from and where is it going? It returns to the mystery whence it came, though terms such as "coming from" and "returning" are inadequate, because they are borrowed from the spatiotemporal world. This mystery is not an absolute nothingness, but one that is relative to human understanding, as thought finds itself unable to explain anything outside of the spatiotemporal world.

The word *mystery* does not therefore denote any entity, it simply indicates the limit of the human spirit's competence.

After the death of the body, the animating impulse, what mysteriously animated this body, does not disappear (again, the image is borrowed from the spatiotemporal world), it returns to the mystery whence it came, and that in fact it never left since manifest life—the appearance—does have, besides its modal and modifiable aspect, a mysterious aspect.

Every human being, no matter what his degree of sublimation or error be, accomplishes—in his real death—a metaphysical resurrection, a return to the mystery.

Metaphysical images aim at sustaining emotion in the face of the mystery of life and death, and at awakening faith in right and in the justice of life. If man mistakes such images for realities, not only does he not calm his anxiety in the face of life and death, but he increases it. In the dogmatic conception of resurrection, the two aspects of resurrection are not distinguished but confused, which deprives each aspect of its genuine meaning, and leads to a superstitious belief in a resurrection after death seen not as a symbolic image but as a reality. If man denies the symbolic scope of these images, he kills his emotion in the face of life and death, he banalizes himself.

Jesus goes on talking about the moral significance of this resurrection:

> 3:8 "The wind blows wherever it pleases;
>   you hear its sound,
>   but you cannot tell where it is coming from or where it is going
>   That is how it is with all who are born of the Spirit."

The wind is the symbol of the creative and animating Spirit, of its breath; it is the essential call. One can hear its voice, feel oneself being called, be "resurrected," straighten up morally under the inner commandment of the spirit, but one "does not know where it comes from or where it is going"; even one who is born of the spirit, "who has been resurrected," does not know where the organization of all that exists comes from and to where it is returning; it "vanishes" in the unfathomable mystery confronting thought when the latter tries to understand the cause and origin of the world and of existence. The introduction of mystery in its impenetrable form in this passage devoted to the moral problem, prepares the introduction of the metaphysical resurrection of which Jesus speaks later on.

Since Nicodemus still does not understand (see verse 9), Jesus says to him,

> 3:10 "You, a teacher in Israel, and you do not know
>   these things!"

Nicodemus persists in his ignorance and becomes so perplexed that he does not even ask any questions; ony Jesus speaks:

> 3:11 "I tell you most solemnly,
>   we speak only about what we know
>   and witness only to what we have seen,
>   and yet you people reject our evidence."

Jesus does not speak lightly; he knows what he says; he has seen what he witnesses to. He knows what the resurrection of the Spirit, the rebirth is, he knows that he has been called and cannot resist the imperative call of the vital impulse, God in man. Such things are quite easy to understand, yet Nicodemus does not understand them; how will he be able to understand when they will have to be broadened to their metaphysical dimension?

> 3:12 "If you do not believe me
>   when I speak about things in this world,
>   how are you going to believe me
>   when I speak to you about heavenly things?"

And, starting to speak about heavenly things, about metaphysical resurrection as we explained it earlier, Jesus brings Nicodemus's perplexity to its climax; he adds these words that for Nicodemus—since he can only understand literally—can only be absurd, incredible:

> 3:13 "No one has gone up to heaven
>   except the one who came down from heaven,
>   the Son of Man who is in heaven."

Only the Son of Man, man *par excellence*, the sanctified man, the man who is fully moved by his essential desire, he who "came down from heaven"—i.e., the only one whose soul-Essence is completely united with the Father-Essence—only he has gone up to heaven, can unite with the Father-Essence, "be one" with the Father, as he will say later, for he alone through the exceptional strength of the symbolically "divine" impulse animating him, is sufficiently purified; he has sublimated, dissolved the multiplicity of his accidental desires and lives only his essential desire, according to its total demand for harmony.

The union of the soul-Essence with the Father-Essence is a symbolic image: Jesus (his soul-Essence) fully takes on himself the mysterious meaning of life (the Father-Essence). There is no contradiction between the evolutionary demand and his own "ego" freed from any vain egocentricity.

Even if he himself—as he stressed to Nicodemus (3:8)—does not know where life comes from, he can still rest, right now, in the "mystery" symbolized by God since he has overcome all his anxiety in the face of the forever unknowable aspect of life; and if he has overcome anxiety it is because he takes on himself the fullness of life's demand: harmony.

"Heaven" is not only joy, reward for awaking from banalization, it is also a metaphysical image, a symbolic reward, the heaven of "the Eternal Presence," the quasi-perfect union of the man

Jesus with the "Essence," with the meaning of life, therefore the elimination of the distance between the soul-Essence and the Father-Essence. Joy can be achieved by any man possessing a strong vital impulse, at least periodically so. The "Eternal Presence" can only be reached by the saint.

> 3:14 "And the Son of Man must be lifted up
> as Moses lifted up the serpent in the desert."

This is a reference to the episode during which Moses talks with Yahweh. Frightened by the mission that his inner impulse (Yahweh) proposes to him, he attempts to get away, pleading an insufficient strength of soul. His impulse replies, quite rightly, that it will be enough "to lift up the serpent in the desert." The serpent is the symbol of vanity in its etymologically deep meaning: the vacuum (see the translation of the myth of Genesis[38]). The desert is the symbol of the banalized world. Moses is perfectly aware of the danger he will face if he obeys this call: he runs the risk of letting himself be trapped in the desire to dominate perversely those he should lead, and to justify his behavior as being the achievement of the meaning of life. He runs the risk that "in his hand," his stick, his scepter received as a sign of his spiritual power, become a serpent, the vanity of banal domination. To this, his impulse replies, "Lift up the serpent . . ." Yes, this could happen to you, but if you are capable of sublimating vanity (of lifting up the serpent), then the serpent will become a scepter in your hands, and you will recover the genuineness of your commandment.

The reference to Moses is not a fortuitous one; Moses is especially dear to the whole Jewish people; evoking his example helps to make Nicodemus pay close attention to Jesus' words: just as vanity can be sublimated as Moses showed, so "the Son of Man must be lifted up" in the heart of those who understand his message: the hope he represents must be accepted, it must become a call to the work of sublimation. The latter is simply the dissolution of vanity, of all vain hopes; now, Nicodemus, like all Jews at that time, hopes to see Jesus free the people from the yoke of the Romans as Moses freed them from the yoke of the Egyptians. Moses was able, at least for a while, to dissolve the vain temptation (he "lifted up the serpent in the desert"); as to Jesus, he does not stop in this task, the essential task of life; he will say later to his disciples: "Now the prince of the world is to be overthrown" (12:31). The prince of the world is the principle ruling the world, vanity. Nicodemus is thus invited to follow the example of Jesus in this work of the sublimation of vanity.

> 3:15 "so that everyone who believes in him may have eternal life in him."

He who has faith in the hope that the man Jesus can represent for every man, he who would accept his proposal, will have "eternal life"; he will live, during his lifetime, according to eternal truth, he will develop in himself essential life as men who accepted the meaning of life, preferring to die in the body rather than dying in the soul, have done it since the most remote times.

This passage, stressing that the condition for salvation is that "the Son of Man be lifted up," magnified in the heart of man, an invitation to dissolve vanity, therefore has no connection with the crucifixion, contrary to what dogmatism has claimed, because there is no real analogy between the lifting up of the serpent and the lifting up on the cross. All the more so since Jesus could not have foreseen at that point, at the start of his mission, that he would be nailed to the cross. An analogy was made after the fact—though it is only a formal one—in an attempt to justify the dogmatic conception of salvation: the mystical redemption by death on the cross. Just as men were not saved by the actual fact of "lifting up the serpent in the desert" (which would, strictly speaking, mean nothing at all), the crucifixion, the lifting up of Jesus on the cross, cannot in itself be the condition for salvation. The condition bringing "salvation," making possible escape from the death of the soul, banalization, is to find in the example of the sanctified man the strength to satisfy one's own essential desire, and thus to tear oneself away from banalization. The exceptional strength of acceptance manifested at the time of the crucifixion is, at most, an event that can reinforce one's trust in the power given by essential life. Had Jesus never been crucified, the sublime elevation of his life would be, for those who understand the essential significance of this life, a sufficient condition for inner rebirth.

Our reference to the myth of redemption was necessary at this point so as to do away with the dogmatic explanation of this passage dealing with the lifting up on the cross, as well as the following passage; in the dogmatic explanation these two passages are seen as including a prophecy of Jesus about his death, at a time when no danger was yet perceivable—a prophecy that is therefore seen as miraculous.

> 3:16 "Yes, God loved the world so much,
>   that he gave his only Son,
>   so that everyone who believes in him may not be lost
>   but may have eternal life."

Life and the world appear, in their mysterious organization, in such an admirable way that they seem to be the fruit of a creator animated by a deep love for creation. And here a man who is capable of taking on himself the meaning of life, of embodying this mysterious organization even to the least details of his thought and feelings, has become a historical reality. This man is the symbolic son of the symbolic Creator. He is in fact an evolutionary product of the mysterious organization of nature, a proof that life can be lived in its fullness, and thereby, a hope for all men to achieve fullness, always in accordance with their individual impulse, to be sure. Faith in the possibility of an essential achievement of each person depending on his strength, makes it possible to attain "salvation" and not to perish in banalization.

> 3:17 "For God sent his Son into the world
>   not to condemn the world,
>   but so that through him the world might be saved."

A man has been able to save himself from essential perdition, banalization of the spirit, by tearing himself away from the conventions and dogmatic beliefs received since childhood; how then does he save the world? By showing in a convincing way— even at the cost of his life—that the satisfaction of life is inner harmony, fidelity to the demands of the spirit, in opposition to the conventionality of thought and the subjection to dogmatic beliefs.

If a man has thus been able to develop the authenticity of his thought while remaining faithful to his vital impulse even unto death, it is in principle, possible for human beings to live in accordance with the truth, whatever the outer conditions that have to be suffered.

3:18 "No one who believes in him will be condemned;
but whoever refuses to believe is condemned already
because he has refused to believe
in the name of God's only Son."

Verse 18 seems to contradict the beginning of verse 17. This is not the case, because the reference is not to an external judgment uttered by a real Being, but to a judgment that is immanent in the psyche itself. Agreement with the self, with the essential desire of harmonization, is the only condition needed for not being subjected to the self-condemnation of guiltiness. Thus, whoever has faith in the possibility of living according to essential desire and lives so insofar as his own strength will permit, will not be subjected to the torture of guiltiness. On the other hand, whoever has no faith in this idea of harmony and, by this very fact, turns away from it, is condemned by his own guilty feelings. He is "already judged."

There is no need to wait for the judgment of a real God, a judgment that would take place after the death of the body or at the time of the Last Judgment, an image that has in fact only a symbolic meaning. Man is judged as soon as he condemns himself to bypass all the essential joys of life.

Thus, faith in the "essence" manifested by faith in the man Jesus, is not faith in a real god, but the certainty that life has a meaning and that this meaning is inner harmonization. Faith in the "essence" is an act. It implies, if it is not to remain merely a dead belief, an intrapsychic work to dissolve the exaltations, a liberation from conventions that are lethal for the life of the spirit. The Synoptic Gospels stress detachment from material goods; such a detachment does not imply renouncing natural and meaningful desires, for that would be a moralizing demand. Only exalted—and therefore unhealthy—desires are concerned.

The importance granted to the essential frees man from excessive accidental preoccupations (see Lk 12:22 and 32). "Set your hearts on his [the Father's] kingdom, and these other things will be given you as well." (Lk 12:31).

3:19 "On these grounds is sentence pronounced:
that though the light has come into the world
men have shown they prefer

darkness to light
because their deeds were evil.
3:20 "And indeed everyone who does wrong
hates the light and avoids it
for fear his actions should be exposed.
3:21 "but the man who lives by the truth
comes out into the light
so that it may be plainly seen that what he does is done in God."

This judgment in which man condemns himself through his essential error is expressed by the teaching and the life of Jesus: the truth has enlightened the world: what is this truth? It is the knowledge of the vital fault, preference given to the accidental in its two forms: exalted material and sexual pleasures and worldly esteem (these are the "evil deeds"). The world has turned away from its fault, it has repressed it vainly and fallen into the "darkness" of the subconscious.

Whoever is enslaved by these "evil deeds" dreads the truth that can show him his error; therefore he dreads the Son of Man, who contrary to him lives in accordance with the meaning of life and does not fear to see his most secret intentions brought to light.

These words show once again how well Jesus knew the secrets of the psychic functioning. Let us recall here verse 25 in chapter 2: "he could tell what a man had in him." Let us also recall the call to introspective work in the episode of the adulterous woman.

CHAPTER 16

The First Public Discourse

Chapter 5 brings the first discourse addressed not to a single man but to the whole world, especially to the Pharisees. With the first contact, a conflict erupts. Jesus has come back from Samaria to Jerusalem. A cure takes place on the Sabbath (see 5:1–16). As far as the Pharisees are concerned, this is a sacrilege. Jesus replies (5:17), "My Father goes on working, and so do I."

For the first time, Jesus publicly proclaims the central truth of his symbolic message: God is his Father. For the offended Pharisees, Jesus' claim adds blasphemy to the sacrilege. The punishment is death, whose threat begins to be felt. Jesus' reply (5:17), "My Father goes on working, and so do I," means that the creative work of the organizing spirit, evolution toward a greater lucidity has never ceased to act throughout creation, and since he is not a more or less pious man but the very expression of the organizing impulse, his good work, a manifestation of the creative essence, cannot be subjected to the law of the Sabbath. Later on, Jesus tells them (7:22–23), "Moses ordered you to practice circumcision—not that it began with him, it goes back to the patriarchs—and you circumcise on the Sabbath. Now if a man can be circumcised on the Sabbath so that the law of Moses is not broken, why are you angry with me for making a man whole and complete on a Sabbath?"

Understand that what I have just done is no less sacred than the circumcision, which you do practice on the Sabbath. This is not how the Pharisees see it; Jesus goes on explaining himself symbolically (verses that are repetitious will be grouped according to their theme).

> 5:19 "I tell you most solemnly,
> the Son can do nothing by himself . . ."

The Son of the Father is the man who is fully animated by essential desire. As such, he can do nothing outside of the expression of the organizing spirit. What the spirit accomplishes in its superconscious form: the organization of the inner world, the Son, faithful to the demand of the superconscious (the Father), does also; he organizes himself, he harmonizes himself thanks to the demand of his superconscious (the Father).

> 5:20 For the Father loves the Son
> and shows him everything he does himself,
> and he will show him even greater things than these
> works that will astonish you.
> 5:21 Thus, as the Father raises the dead and gives them life,
> so the Son gives life to anyone he chooses.

The creative essence (a word that only aims at expressing the mystery of creation) that, for the greater satisfaction of all that exists, organized the world (this is nothing but an image) also created the Son, whose almost perfect inner organization makes of him the Only Son of the Father. This is again symbolized by the love of God for his creature. Speaking biologically, life and its evolutionary finality favored the appearance of this "Only Son of Man."

Greater yet than anything else will be the resurrection from the death of the soul, the power of the Son of Man to tear banalized people (see Lazarus) from their tomb.

The Son, since the strength of his spirit is "incarnate" in his thought and his word, can bring about the awakening of those whose soul is dead. But the Son could not do this if the impulse, the organizing spirit (the Father) had not remained alive in the person to whom the message of Jesus is addressed; this is thanks to the Son, but also thanks to the Father, always present, symbol of the mystery of organization that, on the human plane, is manifested by the superconscious, organizer of the psyche.

> 5:22 "For the Father judges no one
> He has entrusted all judgment to the Son."

The creative Essence is displayed in the form of an inexhaustible gift of life granted to all, it neither judges nor condemns, it gives; the Son is the one who judges. This second part of the verse seems, once again, to contradict the most generally used affirmation: that he did not come to judge. But he is talking about the symbolic judgment whose already explained significance is precisely that no judgment is added to essential death, because the latter carries its judgment, its punishment in itself. The verse explains this: "He has entrusted all judgment to the Son." Jesus is judge because, while being symbolically the Son of God, he is a man like all the others. His achievement—sanctification—is thereby the ideal measure of the possible achievement of man. And the insufficiency of each person must be compared to this quasi-perfect accomplishment, not to bring his collapse into inferiority, but to reduce his vanity and awaken his vital impulse. The Son of Man is thus symbolically a judge, but in fact no actual judgment on the part of the Son of God is added to the sentence to essential death that the banalized man passes on himself.

> 5:23 "so that all may honor the Son
> as they honor the Father.
> Whoever refuses honor to the Son
> refuses honor to the Father who sent him."

This judgment of the Son is therefore a judgment rooted in the meaning of life and inherent in his very being. He is the standard. This shows that the Son participates in the creative Essence not like any other creature—manifestation of the creative mystery—but in a particular way, as a unique manifestation of the creative mystery.

In this sense he deserves to be honored, no less than the creative mystery itself. There is thus an identity between the Son and the Father since the Son, taking on himself at its highest degree the spiritualization-symbolization of desires, achieves a quasi-perfect organization of the psyche.

> 5:26 "For the Father who is the source of life
> has made the Son the source of life."

The same idea is developed here: the identity of the Father with the Son. Life, be it psychic or somatic, comes from the mystery of organization, symbolized by the Father. The Son, by taking upon himself this mysterious organization in the best possible way, fully achieves life and its meaning.

> 5:24 "I tell you most solemnly,
> whoever listens to my words,
> and believes in the one who sent me
> has eternal life
> without being brought to judgment."

Whoever listens to what the Son is proposing and has faith in the creative essence manifested in the mysterious intentionality of the whole of nature, has found eternal truth and will live in accordance with eternal truth. However, one condition must be fulfilled: this faith must not be just an empty word, but an inner activity! The evolutionary intentionality of nature must be accepted by man, through the purification of his intentions; he must personally undertake the evolutionary work accomplished during the thousands of years that came before him and that are an evolution toward greater and greater lucidity. Thus escaping any condemnation, he goes from the death of the soul to the life of the soul. Note that the proposition to go from death to life concerns not the future but the present.

> 5:25 "I tell you most solemnly
> the hour will come—in fact it is here already—
> when the dead will hear the voice of the Son of God,
> and all who hear it will live.
> 5:28 "Do not be surprised at this,
> for the hour is coming
> when the dead will leave their graves
> at the sound of his voice
> 5:29 "those who did good
> will rise again to life,
> and those who did evil, to condemnation."

The dead are the banalized people who, like Lazarus, are shut up in the tomb of their exalted desires and will hear the word of the symbolic Son of God and rise again from the death of the soul. "The hour will come—in fact it is here already" shows that this cannot be the Last Judgment, which will never come, but that Jesus is talking about the historical time when he, as a man, is traveling throughout Palestine to bring the Good News.

Being Spirit incarnate, the sanctified man is "the light of the world": he is manifest truth. Before the truth was manifested in him and through him, before the light appeared, before his voice was raised to wake up the dead, people who lived during that decadent era were hopeless, they lived in the dark; they were in "tombs." Since the appearance of the sanctified man, such times are over. All those who are shut up in their banalization, like dead men in their tombs, hear his voice: the possibility of awakening is given to them, but not all of them will listen; in principle they can all be resurrected. Those who do good will rise again to essential life, those who go on doing evil have indeed heard the essential call but, having repressed it, they are destined to banalization, or to use symbolic terms: to definitive condemnation, to essential death, which is all the more irrevocable that now they know the condition for "salvation." Dogmatism understands these words literally and derives from them the dogma of Resurrection: on the last day, men will hear the voice of God and will rise bodily from their tombs to face their definitive judgment.

> 5:30 "I can do nothing by myself.
> I can only judge as I am told to judge,
> and my judging is just
> because my aim is not to do my own will
> but the will of him who sent me."

As was already stressed in verse 21, the Son does nothing on his own, the spirit Father, the superconscious, the organizing Spirit acts in him; he judges according to what his superconscious dictates to him; therefore his judgment is just; he will not judge as a more or less emotional man but as one who is animated by the essential force and subjected to that essential force.

> 5:31 "Were I to testify on my own behalf,
> my testimony would not be valid.
> 5:32 "but there is another witness who can speak on my behalf
> and I know that his testimony is valid."

The testimony is not given by the accidental being, the emotional one, the vain self—contrary to what happens in the world where, moved by vanity, everyone talks about himself and his actions. When Jesus testifies on his own behalf, his essential being, the Father in him, becomes the veracious witness to his words and deeds.

> 5:33 "You sent messengers to John
> and he gave his testimony to the truth.
> 5:34 "not that I depend on human testimony,
> no, it is for your salvation that I speak of this."

John testified on my behalf (see 1:29 and 30), Jesus tells them, but he is a fallible man, while the Father in me, the superconscious 'tells me all that I should do' and it is that testimony that I am invoking. Your salvation consists in understanding that I am animated by "the spirit of God," the truth, the genuine superconscious demand; it testifies on my behalf and if you understand this, you will be saved.

5:35 "John was a lamp alight and shining
    and for a time you were content to enjoy the light that he gave."

John enlightened you, but his word will not endure because it does not have the power of the immutable truth.

5:36 "But my testimony is greater than John's:
        the works my Father has given me to carry out,
        these same works of mine
        testify that the Father has sent me."

Worthier than John himself are my works, expressing the essential force that animates me: the blind (to the truth) see, the deaf (to the truth) hear, the dead (banalized people) are raised.

5:37 "Besides; the Father who sent me
        bears witness to me, himself.
        You have never heard his voice,
        you have never seen his shape."

The Father is the unfathomable mystery. This verse stresses again the most fundamental condition for any true faith, and without which even faith in the Son who was sent would only be a superstition: the awareness of mystery: "You have never heard his voice, you have never seen his shape." He is the unknowable (see the conversation with Nicodemus, 3:8); emotion in the face of the mystery of life is the indispensable condition for having faith in the Son. For faith in the Son is the unshakable certainty that man must be capable of self-organization—i.e., of self-harmonization—and he must be able to find in this harmonization true satisfaction, since he is an integral part of this mysterious and lawful organization of the existing world. Banalization and essential life are radically opposed. Now the Son has fully assumed the essential dimension of life, he has overcome "the prince of the world," the vain valuations and principles that rule the world. Therefore he represents the hope of being able to overcome banalization. However, in order to understand this, one must have been moved by the mysterious aspect of life and have perceived the vital error of banalization.

And Jesus adds,

> 5:38 "and his words find no home in you
> because you do not believe
> in the one he has sent."

Which means "You have no faith in the Son, the hope that I represent and take upon myself, and therefore the word of truth, the Logos, does not reach you. Yet it would be the only way to awaken in you the awareness of the mystery. The mysterious dimension of life is a reality that is far more obvious than any other; live according to such a reality." But the Pharisees do not have the word of God, the Holy Spirit, the spirit of truth in them; in other words: their essential soul is dead in them. And this is why they are incapable of having faith in Jesus, incapable of understanding that what remains a mystery for the human spirit, the mysterious cause of all that is, is however revealed in the life and works of the Son; by becoming manifest in such a way, the "Father" who sent him, while remaining a mystery, bears witness himself to his son. And Jesus tells the Pharisees,

> 5:39 "You study the Scriptures,
> believing that in them you have eternal life;
> now these same Scriptures testify to me."

The Pharisees could not be more dumbfounded. Like Nicodemus, they have fallen silent, and whatever Jesus adds can only add to their perplexity.

You study the Scriptures, he tells them, and you do not see that they talk only about me, not about me the man Jesus, but about Christ the anointed of the Lord, the truth I embody, the hope of being born again that I assume and bring to you.

This hope has always been foreseen and expected. It is now fulfilled. You should recognize this and come to me to have essential life.

> 5:41 "As for human approval, this means nothing to me.
> 5:42 "Besides, I know you too well:
> you have no love of God in you."

What good would it do to me to receive the approval of men who do not live in the essential?

> 5:43 "I have come in the name of my Father
> and you refuse to accept me;
> if someone else comes in his own name
> you will accept him."

The truth in whose name I come to you does not interest you and you do not hear it. You would accept anybody else because he would talk to you in the conventional ways of the world.

> 5:44 "How can you believe
> since you look to one another for approval
> and are not concerned
> with the approval that comes from the one God!"

The approval, the esteem that you can give to one another can only be a conventional and vain approval since it is not rooted in essential esteem, which proves that you have no faith and that you do not live according to the certainty that the love of truth is a source of joy.

> 5:45 "Do not imagine that I am going to accuse you before the Father;
> you place your hopes on Moses,
> and Moses will be your accuser.
> 5:46 "If you really believe him
> you would believe me too
> since it was I that he was writing about.
> 5:47 "but if you refuse to believe what he wrote,
> how can you believe what I say?"

Moses gave you the law, and you hope to be saved by obeying it. But Moses announced my advent and if you understood what he was talking about, you would have faith in me; but since you do not understand what he said, you do not understand either what I say.

This is no longer a blasphemy against God, which they could just about let go without reacting since Jesus clearly has some power over the people. This is a blasphemy against the Pharisees. No compromise is possible anymore. A merciless war has been declared. Jesus could not behave otherwise unless he wanted to retreat and be silent. Yet he could not deceive himself about the outcome of this war that, on one side, will be fought only with the weapons of the Spirit, and on the other, with all the weapons of temporal power. Jesus is not deceiving himself. Now he knows the outcome and can prophesy it.

To sum up, this chapter clearly shows that the condition for salvation is faith in the one who is symbolically the Son of God, trust in what he affirms: resurrection from the death of the vital impulse, from banalization, is possible, it is even the only real satisfaction. The phrase "to be born in the Spirit," used in the discourse to Nicodemus, has been replaced by the synonymous expression "to resurrect."

CHAPTER 17

The Multiplication of the Loaves

Chapter 6 starts with a brief symbolic scene that is translated in this second part because it would have been difficult to detach it from the teaching it is linked to. The multiplication of the loaves symbolizes the distribution of spiritual food to the world.

> 6:5 Looking up, Jesus saw the crowds approaching and said to Philip: "Where can we buy some bread for these people to eat?"
> 6:6 He only said this to test Philip; he himself knew exactly what he was going to do.
> 6:7 Philip answered: "Two hundred denarii would only buy enough to give them a small piece each."

Jesus tests his disciples. Have they understood what he wants to convey to them? Two is the number symbolizing the appearance and its duality as opposed to the unity of the mystery of organization. It symbolizes, by extrapolation, earthly desires and their promises. The latter can be positive and represent the natural satisfactions of materialism and sexuality; they can also be negative and then symbolize the exaltation of these same desires.

Two hundred denarii represented at that time a very large amount of money: one denarius was the average wage for a day's work.

Thus the earthly food symbolized by two hundred denarii cannot really satisfy the people who have come to listen to Jesus. They hunger for another food, as Philip knows.

> 6:8 One of his disciples, Andrew, Simon Peter's brother, said: "there is a small boy here with five barley loaves and two fish, but what is this between so many?"

The boy is the symbol of the spirit. Being young, he represents the hope of the spirit. Moreover, he has five loaves of barley and two fish. Now, 5 is, in its positive significance, the happy medium, harmony (see page 91). Bread, as we have shown (cf. the Introduction) is the symbol of truth. Barley bread is the bread of the poor: in this respect, it symbolizes the fact that truth is incompatible with the powers of the world. The fish represents banalization (see the Introduction). Taken from the water, it becomes the sublimation of banalization. The two fish are therefore a figure for the sublimation of material and sexual banalization (see our previous explanation about the number 2).

The young boy symbolizes the proposal to feed on spiritual truth and sublimation of the exalted desires. He brings the simplicity of the genuine life of the spirit. But even the disciples do not understand the value of this: "what is this between so many"?

Thus, although on the essential plane the images of the bread and fish are symbolic and deep, on the plane of reality they appear as poor and meager food.

Is this the anxiety of the disciples faced with the conventions of the world? Undoubtedly. But more than this: doesn't it show the insufficient spiritual preparation of a crowd that is not mature enough to receive the message? "What value can the truth have for the world?" is the real question posed by Andrew.

6:11 Then Jesus took the loaves, gave thanks, and gave them out to all who were sitting ready; he then did the same with the fish, giving out as many as were wanted.

Yet Jesus, by attacking error, by stressing the evidence of truth and the certainty of the satisfaction it brings, turns into an inexhaustible abundance what had—at the outset—seemed to be totally inadequate. Hungry spirits can only be fed by a union between sublime achievement and veracious word; i.e., the word being exemplified by the sanctified life (the unique example). This is the true food capable of bringing about in all men faith in life.

Note that symbolism accounts—through these images—for something obvious that is too often forgotten: men cannot possess at the same time the same temporal riches; this is why they quarrel for their ownership. But, together, they can possess the same truth. The more numerous they will be to feed on it, the more powerful it will be in countering error.

6:12 When they had eaten enough, he said to the disciples:
"Pick up the pieces left over, so that nothing gets wasted."
6:13 So they picked them up, and filled twelve hampers with scraps left over from the meal of five barley loaves.

His very disciples, who are cognizant of his teaching, are invited to partake of this food of truth and asked not to waste any of it. Moreover, the teaching that is offered is so tremendous that it is impossible to exhaust its significance. It is an unfailing source. Note that the figure 12 is, in its positive meaning, the number of achievement (the twelve apostles, the twelve tribes of Israel).

6:14 The people, seeing this sign that he had given, said:
"This is really the prophet who is to come into the world."

However, for the people, the awaited prophet remains above all the conquering Messiah, the warrior-king. The people confuse the accidental hope of deliverance from the Roman yoke and the essential hope of attaining the truth. The following verse shows that such was the misunderstanding of the Jewish people and that Jesus was fully aware of it.

The Old Testament shows the Jewish people punished throughout their history through the sanctions inflicted on them by Yahweh, the symbol of immanent justice: the conquest of Samaria by the Assyrians, the conquest of Jerusalem by Nebuchadnezzar, and the captivity in Babylon. It was right to consider the external defeats of the people as the consequence of their disregard for the essential, since forgetting it leads people to banalization and the latter saps courage and destroys combativeness, which means that the people lose their capacity to defend themselves against invaders. On the other hand, when Cyrus, king of Persia, freed the Jewish people, this was considered as a proof that Yahweh had forgiven them. It is therefore not surprising that the Jews, accustomed to seek in accidental happenings manifestations of God's anger against them, or on the contrary proofs of his love, wanted to turn Jesus into the one who, like Moses, would unite the essential mission and external success. In such a view of things, reward and punishment—while being an image of immanent justice—are considered as expressing the merit or error of the whole people.

What Jesus brings is the concept of individual responsibility; his message proposes to each individual—whatever the accidental conditions in which he lives, even if it be in the most extreme banalization—to purify himself from the exaltation of desires and to live in accordance with the essential demand of harmony.

Historical defeats, accidental vicissitudes, revolutions, and wars thus continue to be the punishment of a people or the whole of mankind, forgetful of the essential call; but in this generalized banalization, the individual who does not want to be dragged into the general drift, can save himself from the death of the soul.

> 6:15 Jesus, who could see that they were about to come and take him by force and make him king, escaped back to the hills by himself.

Jesus did not plan to become the king of the Jews, the Messiah according to the flesh. Not that he had not been so tempted (see Lk 4:13 and Mt 4:1–11: the temptations of Jesus[39]).

Going back to the hills is perhaps due not only to the need to escape from this demand of the people, but also to the need to struggle against temptation, to return to elevation, symbolized by the hills, and to face his inner solitude. Jesus' objective is not temporal, it is essential, it is the resurrection from death of the soul, during life.

> 6:16 That evening the disciples went down to the shore of the lake,
> 6:17 and got into a boat to make for Capernaum on the other side of the lake. It was getting dark by now and Jesus had still not rejoined them.

His disciples, already anxious because of the hostile stance of the Pharisees, and frightened by the turn events were taking, flee to the other side of the lake. They are in the night of disorientation, in the inner darkness; hope, represented by Jesus, has left them for a while.

> 6:18 The wind was strong and the sea was getting rough.

The rough sea is the symbol of the inner agitation felt by the disciples (an "inner tempest" is a common phrase) in the face of the dangers that are threatening them.

6:19 They had rowed three or four miles when they saw Jesus walking
on the lake and coming toward the boat. This frightened them.
6:20 but he said: "It is I, do not be afraid."

The symbolic walk on the water takes place when the threats
against Jesus are becoming clearer (see 5:18). The attitude of Jesus expresses his calmness and courage and thus reassures the
frightened disciples, who are terrified about what is in store for
them.

It is interesting to read this text in comparison with Mt 15:24–
32, in which Peter, the most courageous and devoted of the disciples, sinks into anxiety at the prospect of having to face the
attacks of the world that, as he knows, can lead even to death.
In contrast to Jesus, who overcomes the essential danger, Peter,
for his part, is overwhelmed by anxiety, symbolized by the risk
of drowning. Yet the crowd does not give up the vain and dan-
gerously awakened hope: since Moses did indeed free the people
from the power of the Egyptians, why would Jesus not free them
from the Roman yoke? His prophetic mission does seem to direct
him to such an undertaking (cf. 22–25); the people, going after
Jesus, cross the lake and demand the very proof of their hope,
an indisputable miracle such as—according to superstition—
those that Moses had produced. However, Jesus still hopes that
the crowd is drawn to him by a quest for the truth, for he says
to them,

6:26 "I tell you most solemnly
you are not looking for me
because you have seen the signs
but because you had all the bread you wanted to eat."

What joy there must have been in the voice of Jesus when the
crowd he had fed with the multiplied loaves; i.e., to whom he
had offered the essential food, the true bread of life, his truth
and his soul, comes to look for him even on the other side of the
lake of Galilee. The crowd does not affirm the reason for this
quest; he affirms it when talking to the crowd, as if wanting to
convince the people. It is certainly partially true because man is
not only aiming for the accidental. Interest in the truth can also
be awakened. This is confirmed by verse 28:

6:28 Then they said to him: "What must we do if we are to do the works that God wants?"

This is the proof, as has already been said, that the people have been touched by the words of Jesus.

6:29 Jesus gave them this answer: "This is working for God: you must believe in the one he has sent."

Which means, the essential work you have to do is to have faith in the messenger of the eternal truth, to know that the resurrection of the soul during life is possible for man and that, moved by such a faith, he can live essentially.

For if they have no faith in Jesus who revivifies the eternal truth, which is always dogmatized and misunderstood all over again, they remain perforce within a superstitious belief that does not sustain their vital impulse.

Only a renewed formulation that is meaningful for its time can truly move man.

We are presently faced with the same problem: to transpose this message in conceptual terms and to understand symbolism in order to regain the emotion that has been lost due to a literal understanding.

At this point what binds these men to Jesus is the word of truth (the multiplied loaves) that he has given them in abundance.

Note that in verse 26 Jesus counters the signs generally seen as miracles with "all the bread you wanted to eat." This is the indisputable proof that the multiplication of the loaves is not a miracle: otherwise his words would be meaningless. Moreover, if the multiplication of the loaves had actually taken place, no doubt could have remained in people's minds and it is completely impossible that the very same crowd on the following day, after having witnessed such a convincing miracle, could have shouted,

6:30 "What sign will you give to show us that we should believe in you? What work will you do?
6:31 "Our fathers had manna to eat in the desert . . ."

Such a demand is a clear proof that Jesus has not performed the indisputable "miracle"; i.e., one that goes against the laws of physical nature. On the other hand, Moses, according to them, did perform a miracle; now all the miracles that have been performed, the rain of manna or the multiplication of the loaves are only symbolic narratives (this is not so in the case of the healing of hysterical and psychosomatic illnesses). But just as the Jews ended up by believing that the symbolic tales of the Old Testament are indisputable miracles and supreme proofs for their belief, so the Christians came to see the symbolic narratives of the New Testament as indisputable miracles and supreme proof of their belief. The answer given by Jesus (see below) can only destroy the vain hope of the crowd. Hope will give way to disappointment, which will end up in confusion and perplexity. This naive disappointment of the crowd, which will get stronger and stronger with time, will finally become no less dangerous than the hatred of the Pharisees; since Jesus never produces the supreme proof that alone could have convinced the crowd and the Pharisees, he will wind up being crushed between the ignorance of the people and the arrogance of the Pharisees. Instead of producing the miracle that is demanded, Jesus is compelled, not only to disappoint the false belief he arouses in spite of himself, but also to scandalize the crowd by an affirmation that, for them, will only be a new blasphemy:

> 6:32 Jesus answered:
> "I tell you most solemnly,
> it was not Moses that gave you bread from heaven,
> it is my Father who gives you the bread from heaven,
> the true bread.
> 6:33 "for the bread of God
> is that which comes down from heaven
> and gives life to the world."

In order to avoid repetitions, we will regroup the verses according to their themes. Two fundamental themes are intertwined in verses 32 to 65. One deals with essential food, and the other with the metaphysical resurrection. We will treat them separately, so as to give their psychological significance, but in fact they are deeply linked, since the man who receives food for the soul resurrects during life and the reward for this essential rebirth is the sublimation of fear in the face of death. This will be studied at length for verses 39, 40, and 44. To verses 32 and 33—already quoted—we must add,

6:49 "Your fathers ate the manna in the desert
and they are dead.
6:50 "but this is the bread that comes down from heaven
so that a man may eat it and not die."

And again,

6:58 "This is the bread come down from heaven
not like the bread our ancestors ate,
they are dead.
But anyone who eats this bread will live forever."

This concerns, once again, the death of the soul and the life of the soul. The manna that fed the Jewish people symbolizes the word of Moses, as the bread symbolizes here the word of Jesus; had Moses actually brought down a rain of manna in its genuine symbolic significance of essential food, such manna would really be the bread from heaven, the truth. But since it did not prevent the spirits that fed on it from falling back into death—i.e., into banalization—it is obvious that the word of Moses (the manna) was not the authentic bread from heaven given by the "Father," the essential truth (see 6:32).

Moses, in spite of his great vital impulse, failed in his mission; he preferred the success of his people to its essential success, and this at the cost of the blood of other peoples. But "he who eats the true bread from heaven" (see 6:58)—i.e., the soul feeding on real truth, in this case the word of Jesus—is the soul who will never die, who will forever have, during life on earth, eternal truth, eternal life (6:58).

Jesus is the symbolic Son of God; he is the real keeper of the truth, while Moses remained partially subjected to the external success of his people.

This clearly means: only the truth is the source of life; what matters most is not to be freed from the Roman yoke, but to escape from death of the soul, banalization, to feed on "the bread of life," the essential.

6:34 "Sir," they said, "give us that bread always."

This exclamation reveals, on the one hand, their goodwill, but on the other hand, their total inability to understand what Jesus means, since he replies,

> 6:35 "I am the bread of life.
> He who comes to me will never be hungry;
> he who believes in me will never thirst."

After having spoken about the bread come down from heaven, he clearly states,"I am the bread of life"—"my word would amount to nothing if it were not incarnate in me, lived by me, if the example of my entire life were not in conformity with my word, if it did not have the power to make of me the symbolic Son of God. Therefore, I myself have become essential food, capable of satisfying any quest for the meaning of life, of appeasing the hunger and thirst of soul and spirit."

He repeats again in verse 48:

> 6:48 "I am the bread of life. . . ."

This idea is developed at length by Jesus in the following verses:

> 6:51 "I am the living bread which has come down from heaven.
> Anyone who eats this bread will live forever;
> and the bread that I shall give
> is my flesh for the life of the world."
> 6:53 Jesus replied:
> "I tell you most solemnly
> if you do not eat the flesh of the Son of Man
> and drink his blood
> you will not have life in you.
> 6:54 "Anyone who does eat my flesh and drink my blood
> has eternal life
> and I shall raise him up on the last day.
> 6:55 "For my flesh is real food
> and my blood is real drink.
> 6:56 "He who eats my flesh and drinks my blood
> lives in me
> and I live in him.
> 6:57 "As I, who am sent by the living Father
> myself draw life from the Father,
> so whoever eats me will draw life from me."

The bread from heaven is the truth about the fundamental problem of earthly desires, the call to sublimation of exalted earthly desires. This proposal and its achievement bring essential life to the world. But since Jesus has fully taken upon himself this call of the ideal, he himself has become the bread of life; this bread is represented by his sanctified flesh; i.e., by the sublimation of his earthly desires. To feed on this truth is symbolically speaking to eat his flesh. The image of "eating" stresses and concretizes the idea.

To eat human flesh was, from the earliest days of animism, a common and very significant practice[40]: primitive man ate the flesh of the enemies he had vanquished so as to acquire their strength. Little by little, as mores evolved, man freed himself from this primitive practice; it remained only in a purely symbolic form. Jesus has fed with his example men hungering after the truth; being himself purified from any exalted earthly desire, he has proposed to other men to follow his example, to purify their earthly desires, to sublimate their exalted desires. He has offered them the example of his own sublimation, accomplished for his greater joy. He has thus become, in the symbolic formula, "the bread of life." He has nourished them with his blood; i.e., with his soul, his vital impulse, his own faith in the essential. "He who eats this bread will never die." He who frees himself from the exaltation of earthly desires—from banalization—will be saved, he will resurrect during his lifetime, from the death of the soul. His vital impulse has escaped perdition, essential death, banalization. Thus the bread that must be eaten is the sanctified body symbolizing sublime activity, since the Essence has animated every thought, every act in the life of this man Jesus; the phrase "to eat the bread of life" (see 6:54–56), the sanctified body transformed into a symbol of the Essence, is therefore a symbol in itself. Moreover, such a significance is affirmed by Jesus himself in verse 63:

> 6:63 "It is the spirit that gives life
> the flesh has nothing to offer;
> the words I have spoken to you are spirit
> and they are life."

"The letter kills, the spirit only gives life," the apostle Paul will say. "The flesh has nothing to offer" is here contrasted with "the spirit gives life" and signifies understanding limited by vain egocentricity, by love of one's carnal self. In this phrase, "flesh" is understood in a meaning that is antithetical to that of all the preceding verses dealing with the bread of life, the sanctified flesh.

It is therefore necessary above all to understand the spirit in which Jesus taught these verses. Even if he had not been crucified, his "sanctified flesh," symbol of the sublimation of his earthly desires, would have had the same power to "nourish" the spirits hungering for the truth.

The translation of the preceding verses thus enables us to unmask a capital error spread by dogmatism, an error that does not deal directly with the mystery of life, but an error about the essential life of men, about salvation: the error of seeing in the crucifixion the only and real condition for salvation.

The crucifixion is not the miraculous and real cause of salvation; however, Jesus, by preferring actual death to the betrayal of his vital impulse—and this without vanity or complaint—fully accepted the meaning of life: better die in the body than die in the soul, and his death is inscribed in the achievement of his essential desire. In this sense, it is an example for mankind, who so often prefers the satisfaction of earthly desires to the life of the soul, which is a complete inversion of the meaning of life.

Verse 6:51, ending with the affirmation that *"the bread [he] shall give is [his] flesh for the life of the world,"* thus does not in any way refer to the crucifixion. Yet the passage does contain a reference to his death that could be foreseen because of the attitude of the Pharisees and of the people. He offers his "sanctified flesh," the accomplished example, to those who want to receive it as a food, as a promise of possible accomplishment for man; and this is an example for the whole world. To accomplish this offering, his mission, he will not back away from those who will kill his actual body. But the Jews, who were unable to understand and grumbled when he said that he was "the bread come down from heaven" (See 6:41), do not understand either "the offering of his flesh," the example he proposes, and they discuss among themselves:

> 6:52 Then the Jews started arguing with one another:
> "How can this man give us his flesh to eat?"

The Jews of old did not want to admit the symbolic divinity of Jesus; the religious dogmatism of the following centuries did not understand the meaning of this symbolic phrase, which becomes so clear when one has the key to it.

And all that will be added by Jesus (6:53–58), who reiterates "the offer of his flesh," in lieu of the manna that Moses gave, will serve only to turn the disappointment of the people into rancor and their puzzlement into astonishment. Even his disciples, when the people—having given up the idea of making him a king—went away, grumble among themselves:

> 6:60 "This is intolerable language. Who could accept it?"

Truly, this is proof of their lack of understanding.

> 6:42 "Surely this is Jesus, son of Joseph," they said. "We know his father and mother. How can he now say: "I have come down from heaven?"

is a verse that shows how the fact of knowing Jesus prevents them understanding his teaching. The proverb holds true: "No man is a prophet in his own country."

Jesus asks them, "does this upset you?" and he adds the words we have already quoted:

> 6:63 "It is the spirit that gives life
> the flesh has nothing to offer.
> The words I have spoken to you are spirit
> and they are life."

Thanks to the psychological understanding of the preceding verses, one is bound to conclude that the verse

> 6:62 "What if you should see the Son of Man ascend to where he was before?"

is an interpolation. The meaning of the Gospel, and therefore also of its translation, are of one piece and, in conformity with the methodology, any passage that cannot be incorporated into the whole is to be considered as having been interpolated. Now this verse cannot be incorporated. This verse does not deal with the symbolic image of a metaphysical heaven, but with a man-God who rises in body to a heaven located outside space. This reference to a future ascension (6:62) does not refer to the state of essential concentration through which the Son of Man, deep in ecstasy and fulfillment, rises up. The disciples must often have seen Jesus in such a state and no matter how surprising such a state of perfect concentration must have seemed to them, it would certainly not be the factor that would convince them that the disconcerting words just uttered by Jesus are true. Even if we admit that the disciples, to whom this verse is addressed, are half-believers, belonging to the crowd—and not those who usually accompany him—the attempt to convince through such a reminder remains inefficacious. The verse is a reference to the dogma of the miraculous and bodily ascension, conceived much later and in contradiction with the genuine meaning of the Gospel. The words that Jesus addresses to the disciples (6:61–65) can only be incorporated in the true meaning of the Gospel if one eliminates the incriminated verse (6:62), the sentence that—although it is unfinished—is complete for the one who interpolated it since it contains all that he wanted to insinuate. What Jesus meant to say is, you are upset by my discourse; but it upsets you only because you do not want to recognize in me the genuine symbolic Son of God, and by this very fact you do not accept my message. What the interpolator wants to insinuate is my discourse, no matter how surprising it might seem to you, must be understood literally and there is nothing upsetting in it because you will see things that are far more surprising. One day, you will see me go up to heaven in my body. The interpolation is therefore in total contradiction with the true words of Jesus. By telling them, "The spirit gives life, the flesh has nothing to offer" (6:63), Jesus wants to reduce the doubts of his disciples and to show them the way to true understanding. As to the interpolator, he wants to eliminate the doubts that a Christian reader would have in the face of a literal interpretation of this verse; he wants to remind the reader that, in order to be a genuine Christian, one must not be afraid of understanding and believing according to the letter for if one were upset by this relatively innocuous discourse, where then could one find enough strength to believe meekly in things that are far more incredible? Better not to start doubting. This verse is an attempt to prove the incredible by the absurd (the Church will wind up with the "*Credo quia absurdum*") and is therefore clearly shown to be a late addition.

Jesus does not manage to calm the doubt of the Jews:

6:66 After this, many of his disciples left him and stopped going
with him.

As to the interpolator, he did manage to calm for a long time
the doubt of Christians. It must be said, though, that the Church
is now in serious difficulty, but the dogma of the resurrection of
bodies still endures.

We will broach now the second theme of this long passage:
metaphysical resurrection, which we have already evoked.

6:40 "Yes, it is my Father's will
that whoever sees the Son and believes in him
shall have eternal life,
and that I shall raise him up on the last day."

The man who has faith in the Son and lives in this life in
accordance with the eternal truth, "shall be raised up on the last
day."

This is not a resurrection of the body or of the spirit. This
means a "return" after death, to the unfathomable mystery from
which life emerged.

Only an image can express this aspect of the problem: as a
drop of water rises in the air when projected by a wave and then
returns to the immensity of the sea and remains extant, though
is an integral part of the sea, so the individual being, vital impulse of animation, differentiated and individualized during the
brief span of a life, "returns" through his bodily death to the
mysterious ocean of the creative Essence.

This return to the "mystery" is metaphysical resurrection.
Only on the last day of his bodily life, the last day of his appearance that—for anyone who is dying—is the last day of any appearance, only on that last day will man be fully united to the
"Essence," this being understood of course as an image once
again. Each one of us achieves his "return to the mystery,"
whether he has lived well or badly. In what way then is the
intervention of the Son presented as being necessary? Faith in
the Son—faith in the essential, exemplified by the Son—leads to
moral resurrection. The latter is a work of inner healing, inner
purification, accomplished during temporal life. This work and
the capacity to do it vary from one person to the other. And this

is what the symbolic word means: 14:2 "There are many rooms in my Father's house . . ."

There are different degrees in the intensity of the essential impulse that is symbolically expressed by a varying distance from the mysterious "Essence." The symbolic image of the union of the soul-Essence with the Father-Essence, almost perfectly achieved by the man Jesus, awakens in other men the hope for an essential union that, while it is not perfect, is nonetheless still satisfying, since it is in keeping with the level of each individual. Thus, the people in whom this hope is incarnate "do not die but have eternal life," they live in the eternal truth.

Purification from the exaltation of desires, moral resurrection, is the means to overcome anxiety in the face of death because what unites life to death is a mysterious aspect common to both: if man resurrects during his lifetime, he partakes of the essential, he is then certain that the death of the body is not a cause for anxiety but that it will free him more definitely from the accidental, will enable him to return more fully to the "organizing Essence" from which he came.

The difference between one who is already "resurrected" in his lifetime and one who is not, is that the former lives in certainty while the latter remains in a state of more or less repressed anxiety. The certainty of the mysterious dimension of life, the certainty that life is an unfathomable mystery, the certainty that life is subject to no less mysterious lawfulness, make life something to be lived with enthusiasm and joy. Therefore he who is resurrected in the soul during his life fears nothing. His death will only be the continuation of his quest and its fulfillment: the return to mystery whose dimension he grasped during his lifetime.

The misunderstanding of the Christian myth, which makes the resurrection after death a survival of the spirit coming before a bodily resurrection on the day of the Last Judgment, is a complete aberration.

Jesus unveiled what the esoteric religions taught their initiates. But he did so in a clearer way for those who understood the symbolic language: "The essential is the true dimension of existence, it links the mystery of life and the mystery of death. If you live in the essential, you live outside the temporal, and death and its anxiety have no sway over you." Symbolically speaking, "You will return to the Father from whom you came, do not be anxious."

"The more you live in the essential, the less you will be afraid to leave the accidental and the more you will understand that death is the prolongation of what you were searching for during your entire life." This is not therefore only an appeasement of the anxiety caused by death, it is also enthusiasm for life that, when it is lived in its essential dimension, becomes a constant source of joy.

It is therefore vital to understand the importance of this concept of "metaphysical resurrection" and its link with moral resurrection, as well as the role of the "Son" associated with it.

"Moral resurrection" enables man to develop in himself certainty in the face of the mystery of existence, and thus certainty of "metaphysical resurrection," and the latter in turn calls for a work of purification, during life, of exalted desires.

As to the "Son," he is the unique example, the living incarnation of the meaning of life, the expression of the mystery of organization. The consequence of this is faith in mystery and therefore faith in "metaphysical resurrection."

But all is lost if this "metaphysical resurrection" is seen as a reality; it is only an image—let us repeat it—without any factual content. Thus, this moral resurrection being inspired by his example, Jesus can say,

> 6:37 "All that the Father gives me will come to me
> and whoever comes to me
> I shall not turn him away,
> 6:38 "because I have come from heaven
> not to do my own will,
> but the will of the one who sent me.
> 6:39 "Now the will of the one who sent me
> is that I should lose nothing
> of all that he has given to me,
> and that I should raise it up on the last day."

The fundamental meaning of the sanctified man's life is not to give himself to the world, but to give himself to "the Essence" (see 6:38)—i.e., to concentrate in the essential—and he gives himself to "the Essence" in moments of fullness, in calm and sublime moments when all that is accidental, all that is temporal, loses all importance for him, when his soul-Essence is totally present in the awareness of the unfathomable mystery of existence, he lives in the "heaven" of the "Eternal Presence" and it is from this heaven that he must come down, it is this inner state that he must leave to fulfill his earthly mission; i.e., to bring the word of truth.

> 6:39 "Now the will of him who sent me
> is that I should lose nothing
> of all that he has given me
> and that I should raise it up on the last day.
> 6:44 "No one can come to me
> unless he is drawn by the Father who sent me
> and I will raise him up on the last day."

Those that the "Father," the mysterious intentionality, "gives" him are the people in whom essential desire is strong enough to be animated anew. They are those who come to him "drawn by the Father," drawn by the call of their own vital impulse (see 6:37, 39, 44). But this call is made through the personality of Jesus, who, through his example and words, is capable of awakening men to the essential during their lifetime.

The superconscious demand, "the Father who sent him," obliges Jesus to tear himself away from the inner fullness he lives in the calm of a retreat and to seek union with all men. It is love for his brothers, since they too are animated by essential desire; it is this love, purified from any affect, that would like to awaken them to the life of the soul.

He obeys the "commandment of his Father" (see 6:38–40), the demand of his own impulse, and seeks union with those who, on the basis of their own impulse, are drawn to him; thus they will be united in the same quest, they will commune in the same ideal: the purification of desires. In conformity with the will of the "Father"—i.e., to the extent that they obey the demand of essential desire, the superconscious—they will not be able to get lost anymore. On the other hand, those who cannot feed on the example of Jesus, because they are not animated by a sufficiently strong essential desire, hate him. He "gives his flesh," (see 6:51) must therefore be understood with an additional significance: his essential love is not discouraged by the hatred of men who are essentially dead, by their lethal threat. He will therefore prefer to die (to give his flesh) rather than betray his soul. Dogmatism will see here a prophetic reference to the crucifixion, deemed to be the condition for salvation.

Seeing the perplexity caused by his words, Jesus repeats,

> 6:43 "Stop complaining to each other
> 6:44 "No one can come to me
> unless he is drawn by the Father who sent me
> and I will raise him up on the last day.
> 6:45 "It is written in the prophets:
> *They will all be taught by God*
> and to hear the teaching of the Father
> and learn from it,
> is to come to me."

Verse 44 has already been translated. The prophets said that "they will all be taught by God" (see 6:45); i.e., that the superconscious, the divine in man, exists in each individual and enables him to obtain genuine satisfaction, whatever the accidental givens of his life might be.

This is why one who heeds the call of essential desire can come to the Son. Such a man has heard "the teaching of the Father," the call of the superconscious, though he has not "seen" the Father.

> 6:46 "Not that anybody has seen the Father
> except the one who comes from God:
> he has seen the Father."

This verse is not in contradiction with the Prologue (see Jn 1:18): "No one has ever seen God." In the Prologue, God is the symbol of the unfathomable mystery that no one, not even the sanctified man, can penetrate. However, "the man of God," the man who is totally animated by essential desire—i.e., the one who has completely sublimated his personal desires to assume the evolutionary vital impulse—that one "has seen the Father." This image symbolizes the permanent and active emotion in the face of the organizing mystery, but not the understanding of the unfathomable mystery of life. The fullness of such an emotion can be achieved only by the sanctified man when he is united with the "Essence"—a mystical union—which, on the psychological plane, means freedom from any accidental desire and total concentration in essential desire, and this is impossible for anyone except a saint (Jesus and Buddha can be called saints). At such moments, he has—as he himself puts it—"seen" the Father, and at such moments the Father "tells" him what he must do.

He who has "seen the Father" lives in "the Eternal Presence," which is another symbolic expression. This was brought out in the conversation with Nicodemus. "The Eternal Presence" of God in the man Jesus has only a symbolic significance. He has grasped the mysterious dimension of life, it is constantly present in him. Any other man, more or less subject to the sway of vanity, remains in an ambivalent state in the face of the essential: drawn but with more or less anxiety.

The deepest cause of the dogmatic superstition is that, while talking about mystery, people end up misunderstanding the meaning of the word and wanting to explain speculatively that which—by its very definition—remains unexplainable. The speculative dogmatization of mystery leads to the disappearance of the true object of any genuine faith: the mystery of the world and of all life; this is the cause of the transformation of faith into dead belief, and all the speculative errors simply follow on from this one.

CHAPTER 18

Threats of the World

Verse 6:67 is pregnant with significance:

6:67 Then Jesus said to the Twelve: "What about you, do you
want to go away too?"
6:68 Simon Peter answered: "Lord, who shall we go to? You have the
message of eternal life.
6:69 "and we believe; we know that you are the Holy One
of God."

Peter, he whose faith is the best rooted, the most solid, shows
in these verses that he is already certain; he has understood the
true dimension of Jesus, he knows that he incarnates the truth
about the meaning of life and that he fully lives this dimension.
He knows that this man is the saint of God, the Christ (see Mt
16:16), the anointed of the Lord, all these phrases meaning the
same thing: i.e., the man who is totally filled with the essential
emotion, the evolutionary ideal incarnate in a man.

6:70 Jesus replied: "Have I not chosen you, you Twelve? Yet, one
of you is a devil."

I chose all twelve of you, and yet human weakness is such
that among you, who are the most fitted and the best prepared
to understand, there will still be one who will stand against me.
After the teaching on "the bread of life,"

7:1 Jesus stayed in Galilee; he could not stay in Judaea, because
the Jews were out to kill him.

But this retreat is not a cowardly flight, since shortly thereafter, during the Feast of the Tabernacles, Jesus comes back to

the very focus of danger, Jerusalem (7:10). He gives two short discourses (7:16–24, 28–29, 33–36) that bring nothing essentially new. Verses 7:33–34 are repeated in 8:21 and will be translated along with chapter 8. We only wish to stress the translation of the following two verses:

> 7:28 "Yes, you know me and you know where I came from.
> Yet I have not come of myself;
> no, there is one who sent me and I really come from him,
> and you do not know him.
> 7:29 "but I know him
> because I have come from him
> and it was he who sent me."

They know that he is Jesus of Nazareth, son of the carpenter. Yet, it is not as such that he comes to teach to them; he comes as an essential witness to life and to its meaning of which they have no inkling because they are not aware of its mysterious dimension. Therefore he will be able to say just as truthfully,

> 8:14 ". . . you do not know
> where I come from or where I am going." (See chapter 7.)

The Pharisees want to have him arrested, but their police dare not seize him (see 7:44 and 46).

CHAPTER 19

The Testimony

Chapter 8 revolves around the question that the Pharisees are going to ask him: "Who are you?"

> 8:12 "I am the light of the world;
> anyone who follows me will not be walking in the dark;
> he will have the light of life."

Which means, I enlighten the world about its essential destiny; whoever follows me will not walk in the darkness of error, but he will have the light of truth. To know "who he is," it is sufficient not to be blind; one must understand what it is about. The Pharisees, blind and incapable of emotion, demand an external testimony. In accordance with the Judaic Law, only the testimony of two men is worthy of faith.

> 8:13 At this the Pharisees told him: "You are testifying on your own behalf; your testimony is not valid."

But Jesus answers,

> 8:14 "It is true that I am testifying on my own behalf,
> but my testimony is still valid,
> because I know
> where I came from and where I am going;
> but you do not know
> where I come from and where I am going."

He knows that he comes from the mystery and is going back to it, because he does not forget the organization that animates him and that his whole psyche manifests lawfulness; as to the Pharisees, they do not know where he comes from or where he is going because they have forgotten the genuine meaning of life. The testimony of Jesus is rooted in "the eternal truth," and this is what they, the blind, the Pharisees, are unable to understand.

> 8:15 "You judge by human standards;
> I judge no one."

[The French version uses a phrase that translates into English as "you judge according to the flesh"; hence the following passage must be based on the wording of the French version and not the Jerusalem Bible.]

Here the flesh is not flesh in its positive meaning, the sanctified flesh of the man Jesus, symbol of the sublimation of earthly desires, but flesh in its negative significance as opposed to spirit; i.e., attachment to earthly desires, affect.

Jesus thus told them: you judge according to your affect, your conventional assumptions.

> 8:16 "but if I judge
> my judgment will be sound,
> because I am not alone;
> the one who sent me is with me.
> 8:17 "and in your Law it is written
> that the testimony of two witnesses is valid.
> 8:18 "I may be testifying on my own behalf
> but the Father who sent me is my witness too."

Jesus does not want to be supported by the testimony of a man, but only by that of the sole condition for a genuine faith. Moreover, if the Pharisees demand another witness, there is one: the Essence itself, "the Father who sent him," testifying on his behalf. For there is a conformity between what Jesus says and does and the organizing demand that every man knows superconsciously. However, to understand this, one must have experienced essential life. But the Pharisees listen without hearing, without understanding the significance of the answer that Jesus has just given them; they pursue their questioning:

> 8:19 "Where is your Father?"

Then, seeing that the Pharisees will never be able to understand, Jesus replies,

> 8:19 ". . . you do not know me, nor do you know my Father;
> if you did know me, you would know my Father as well."

The answer therefore means, You want to know where the Father is without understanding who is the Son, and this is impossible because one does not go without the other. The Son, through the level of essential organization he is revealing, is the most perfect manifestation of the organizing intentionality (the "Father") who, for a great many people, remains hidden because of the excessive importance granted to the accidental.

Either you understand both the Father and the Son—Jesus tells them or you understand neither one nor the other. Since the testimony that the Son gives by himself is not enough for you, since the light cannot enlighten your inner life, your soul, you will never understand the second witness you are asking for. Since you will never understand, you are going to kill me. Which is why he adds,

> 8:21 "I am going away; you will look for me
> and you will die in your sin.
> Where I am going you cannot come."

Every step I take leads me even closer to the love of the essential, while you will remain until death in the love of the accidental that is blocking your understanding.

But this verse also means, I am going to my death, and by this very fact, I am returning to the mystery but such a word has no emotional echo in you.

This idea had already been expressed in 7:33 and 34.

Verse 8:22 shows the incomprehension of the Pharisees. Yet Jesus goes on:

> 8:23 "You are from below; I
> am from above.
> You are of this world;
> I am not of this world."

He is obviously not talking about celestial space, but about the flat and conventional life of the Pharisees. Therefore his words are meant to convey to the Pharisees that in order to know "who he is", their soul, which is from below, too subjected to accidental desires, should free itself. Jesus does not belong to this world of banalization where the Pharisees live. "His kingdom is not of this world," his world is that of the essential. But the soul of the Pharisees cannot rise because they only see in Jesus the accidental man: "Is he not the son of Joseph?" (6:42) and not the sanctified Son who, because he raises souls toward essential satisfactions, is the Messiah. This is why Jesus repeats,

> 8:24 "I have told you already: you will die in your sins.
> Yes, if you do not believe that I am He,
> you will die in your sins."
> 8:25 . . . "Who are you?"

The deaf and blind Pharisees do not understand that from the outset of his teaching, Jesus has again and again explained to them "who he is" since he has told them substantially that he is an essential manifestation of life and its evolutionary finality, that he is purified flesh, achieved example; after so many explanations, they ask the very same question to which Jesus has already replied. The question proves most decisively that they are totally incapable of understanding the language of the essential. Jesus therefore replies,

> 8:25 "What I have told you from the outset."

meaning "I am the light" (see 8:12), "I am from above" (see 8:23),
> and he adds,

> 8:26 "About you I have much to say
> and much to condemn. . . ."

This is a condemnation that is only echoing the essential sentence they have passed on themselves because of their inability to understand. He goes on,

> ". . . but the one who sent me is truthful,
> and what I have learned from him
> I declare to the world."

Thus they are judged by the "Essence," the Father, the second witness they asked for, the truthful witness who sent him; which means that they are condemned by their own superconscious, the inner demand for harmonization.

As to Jesus he only tells the world "what he has learned from the Father" (8:26); i.e., what his essential desire, freed from any darkness, has been able to tell him. But the Pharisees still do not understand (see 8:27) that he is unceasingly talking about the "Father," the second witness against them. And it is then, in the face of this abysmal incomprehension, that Jesus, cutting it short and summing up his discourse, tells them about his elevation:

> 8:28 "When you have lifted up the Son of Man,
> then you will know that I am He . . ."

As if he wanted to say, "No use repeating myself, you will never understand. You keep your eyes shut firmly lest the light enter. Open your eyes, let the light enter, 'lift up the Son of Man' in your soul, put at the center of yourselves what the Son of Man proposes to you, his teaching and his example, and it is only then that you will understand that the mystery of the organization is not just an empty word: the Son of Man has done nothing but spiritualize and sublimate his desires; i.e., he has organized himself."

To know who he is and to have faith in him is the same thing. We come back therefore to the condition for salvation. The final affirmation, "I have to be lifted up for man to know who I am," talks about the "lifting up of the Son" in the soul of the man of faith; i.e., the enlightment of the soul who has faith in the essential. How can one understand who this man is and the hope he brings, without a sufficient awakening of the vital impulse for it to become receptive to his message?

All the preceding explanations deal with the inner lifting up, thus of the true faith as the condition for salvation; it is therefore clear that the final explanation, supporting the preceding ones, cannot mean the external lifting up, the crucifixion. And because these words about the lifting up have such a meaning and not that of the crucifixion, Jesus can, in conformity with the whole meaning of his discourse, go on summing up and reiterate what he was saying by stressing that these words are veracious, even if he testifies on his own behalf, because

> 8:28 ". . . I do nothing by myself;
> what the Father has taught
> me is what I preach."

And he can add,

> 8:29 "he who sent me is with me,
> and has not left me to myself,
> for I always do what pleases him."

His words and his actions, his deeds, are dictated to him by the superconscious. This is why he is not left to himself. The Father, the superconscious guide, is always with him in his deliberation.

This passage deals therefore with inner elevation, with the elevation of the soul to essential life and the affirmations of Jesus incorporated in this context are not isolated affirmations, but constitute, through their renewed symbolic formulation, a variation and deepening of the central theme of all the Gospels: faith in the essential and its consequences, the condition for salvation.

Jesus goes on:

> 8:32 "you will learn the truth
>   and the truth shall make you free."
> 8:33 They answered: "We are descended from Abraham and have never been the slaves of anyone, what do you mean, 'You will be made free'?"

Once again, they understand according to the letter. The real freedom of which Jesus is speaking is that given by truth about life, its meaning, and consequently, truth about oneself, a new call to work on introspection; for it is in the meaning of life to understand that the mysterious organization of the whole of nature that man is witnessing becomes for him an invitation to organize himself. But whoever is "a slave to sin," under the sway of the exaltation of desires, the overvaluation of accidental satisfactions, loses his "freedom"; he must obsessively justify his exalted desires in order to free himself from guiltiness; and obsession is the contrary of freedom. And this is why the truth makes people free.

> 8:35 "Now the slave's place in the house is not assured,
>   but the son's place is assured.
> 8:36 "So if the Son makes you free,
>   you will be free indeed."

If you go back to the message of the Son, the essential hope he brings, you will become free from sin and its slavery and will be true masters of yourselves, you will also be the sons of the Father and not slaves of sin.

> 8:37 "I know that you are descended from Abraham;
>   but in spite of that you want to kill me
>   because nothing I say has penetrated into you."

Even though you are from the race of Abraham and this is enough for you, it is quite obvious that you do not really understand what I am talking about; I am talking about inner freedom, liberation from obsessions, excessive accidental preoccupations. If you understood this, you would not be seeking to kill me.

> 8:38 "What I, for my part, speak of
> is what I have seen with my Father;
> but you, you put into action
> the lessons learned from your father."

I am testifying for the essential and you witness to error, for your father is the devil, Jesus tells them quite clearly in verse 8:44.

8:39 They repeated: "Our father is Abraham." Jesus said to them:
"If you were Abraham's children,
you would do as Abraham did.
8:40 As it is you want to kill me
when I tell you the truth
as I have learned it from God;
this is not what Abraham did.
8:41 "What you are doing is what your father does." "We were not born of prostitution," they went on, "we have one father: God."
8:42 Jesus answered:
"If God were your father, you would love me
since I have come here from God; yes, I have come from him;
not that I came because I chose,
no, I was sent, and by him.
8:43 "Do you know why you cannot take in what I say?
It is because you are unable to understand my language."

They call Abraham as their witness, but Jesus tells them, Abraham, who was a just man, would not have done what you are doing. If God, as you claim, were your Father, if you were faithful to the essential, you would be aware that I am the very expression of the essential, and you would understand me.

From this passage, it is obvious that when the Pharisees are shocked by the divine filiation of Jesus it is not because Jesus claims to be the real son of God, but because they, the Pharisees, are the true "sons of God." It is quite obvious that they do not claim to be real sons of God, thus they believe themselves to be symbolic sons of God since they are the guardians of the truth, they obey the Law of Moses in its most minute details; as to Jesus, he is "possessed by a demon," he abolishes the Law.

> 8:44 "The devil is your father
> and you prefer to do what your father wants.
> He was a murderer from the start;
> he was never grounded in the truth;
> there is no truth in him at all;
> when he lies
> he is drawing on his own store
> because he is a liar and the father of lies."

The devil is, in the symbolism of the Christian myth (see the temptations of Jesus)[41], the symbol of the vain distortion of the three drives. Represented with horns and the feet of a he-goat (symbol of sexual perversion), the tail of a wolf (symbol of material banalization), a lolling tongue (symbol of false justification, the perversion of the spirit), he is the animal man; i.e., man fallen down to the level of the beast, the banalized man greedy for enjoyment and power, seductive and lying. The Pharisees are therefore sons of the devil, as Jesus is the Son of God. They want to satisfy their banalized desires as he satisfies his essential desire.

Since the beginning of the world, the perverse desires of men have been killing their deep vital impulse. Vanity (the devil) is essentially the contrary of truth, because it is the false justification of exalted desires, the lie about life.

> 8:45 "But as for me, I speak the truth,
> and for that very reason,
> you do not believe me."
> 8:46 "Can one of you convict me of sin?
> 8:47 "A child of God
> listens to the words of God;
> if you refuse to listen,
> it is because you are not God's children."

Fools that you are, you trust the liar in yourselves, the false spirit, and I, consequently, cannot gain your trust because you ignore, you repress, you kill your own essential desire.

> 8:48 The Jews replied: "Are we not right in saying that you are
> a Samaritan and possessed by a devil?"

8:49 Jesus answered:
"I am not possessed,
no, I honor my Father,
but you want to dishonor me."

Jesus is accused of being a Samaritan, and as such abhorred by the Jews. Which means that he is outside of the Jewish community and its covenant with God. He is even accused of being possessed by a demon; i.e., subjected to the spirit of evil. Yet, if Jesus honors the Holy Spirit—which is, let us repeat it again, the evolutionary spirit organizing matter, manifest in all that is—if he is its servant, he is led to oppose all that is conventionally admitted and recognized, he is led to denounce the errors of the dogmatism of his time. Therefore he is seen as the enemy to crush. He is attacked from all sides. "In the eyes of the world, the wise man is mad," says Chinese wisdom.

8:50 "Not that I care for my own glory,
there is some one who takes care of that and is the judge of it.
8:51 "I tell you most solemnly,
whoever keeps my word
will never see death."

Again, he says that he does not seek his own glory, the glory of the accidental self, but the glory of the essential self, the divine in man; whoever follows him in this essential quest will never fall into banalization, symbolized by death.

8:52 The Jews said: "Now we know for certain that you are possessed. Abraham is dead and the prophets are dead, and yet you say: 'Whoever keeps my word will never know the taste of death.'
8:53 "Are you greater than our father Abraham who is dead? The prophets are dead too. Who are you claiming to be?"

Whether they be in good or bad faith, the Jews interpret his words literally, claiming that he is the liar since it is obvious that everybody, even Abraham, is subject to the law of death.

The Pharisees, whose thinking is beclouded by their vanity, are deaf men who want to remain deaf, for it is quite obvious that if Jesus used that language, it was because he knew that it could be understood; the Pharisees, brought up in the culture of the Old Testament, were prepared to understand that he spoke about the death of the soul. A few examples will suffice to convince the reader.

Ps 56:13 ". . . for you have rescued me from Death
to walk in the presence of God
in the light of the living."

Prv 10:2 Right conduct brings delivery from death.

Ez 18:27 When the sinner renounces sin to become law-abiding
and honest, he deserves to live.

Ez 18:28 He has chosen to renounce all his previous sins; he
shall certainly live; he shall not die.

The Pharisees want to use the words of Jesus as the very
proof of his pretentious vanity.

8:54 Jesus answered:
"If I were to seek my own glory
that would be no glory at all;
my glory is conferred by the Father,
by the one of whom you say, 'He is our God,'
8:55 "although you do not know him.
But I know him,
and if I were to say: I do not know him,
I should be a liar as you are liars yourselves.
But I do know him and I faithfully keep his word."

Jesus tells them that his words are not vain, but true, since
vanity and truth are mutually exclusive. Either the Jews are right,
or Jesus is right. Either their "Father" is "God," or "God" is the
"Father" of Jesus, and if this is the case, the "father" of the Jews
is "the devil." See also verses 7:27 and 28, previously translated.

8:56 "Your father Abraham rejoiced
to think that he would see my Day.
He saw it and was glad."

The "day" of Jesus is the day of essential life, the day of joy.
Abraham was a man who, being capable of feeling such a joy,
was aware of the call of essential desire. The understanding of
the image of the "Eternal Presence" (see page 162) enables us to
translate verse 8:58, which is far more enigmatic.

8:57 The Jews then said: "You are not fifty yet, and you
have seen Abraham!"
Jesus replied:

8:58 "I tell you most solemnly
before Abraham ever was,
I Am."

In order to understand this image, the translation itself can only offer an image. If one calls all the psychic functions *psyche* and the mystery of animation *soul*, it follows that only the soul is essentially (and symbolically) speaking immortal. The more man, through his accidental desires, is subjected to the attraction of the world, the less intense his essential life is. According to the metaphysical image, the degree of intensity of satisfaction is given by the image of the distance between psyche and soul.

In the case of the sanctified man, there is no difference between the apparent individuality, the psyche, and the essential soul. His psyche is the perfect manifestation of his essential soul. Jesus, the sanctified man, can thus say truthfully that before the advent of Abraham, he is. He is the eternal truth. Abraham lived in the temporal, while he lives in the "Essence," or, rather, the eternal truth lives in him; therefore, speaking symbolically, he has been living since the beginning of time. The mystery of the organization "is"; it has been manifested since the beginning of time.

Through his life, Abraham manifested his emotion in the face of the mystery and its lawful expression symbolized by Yahweh; this is why he rejoiced at the thought of those who would come after him and would also live according to the essential. The end of this discourse shows (8:59), as do all the discourses in the Gospel of John (5:46, 6:60–61, 7:34, 10:18), that the people do not understand, that they are totally perplexed. This perplexity, in this chapter, as in chapter 10, is stressed by the fact that the Jews pick up stones to cast them at Jesus (8:59, 10:31). Stoning has a symbolic meaning. As we have seen, stoning is a form of crushing by the earth (in the guise of stones), a symbol of the punishment of banalization. Among the Jews, stoning is not only the punishment for adultery, but also for blasphemy, for the profanation of the divine, an extreme form of banalization. The uncomprehending perplexity brought about by the words of Jesus is so extreme that the Jews want to inflict—what an irony!—the punishment for banalization, the symbolic punishment of the death of the soul, on the unique man who raises his voice only in order to call the banalized souls to essential life.

CHAPTER 20

The Dogmatic Error

Chapter 10 starts with the allegory of the Good Shepherd, easy to follow and needing no new explanations. It is followed by a discussion between Jesus and the Pharisees, which is sufficient in itself to demolish the whole structure of dogmatism.

10:24 The Jews gathered around him and said: "How much longer are you going to keep us in suspense? If you are the Christ, tell us plainly."

In order to ask this question, the Jews must think that he is the Christ; to which Jesus replies, I have told you: I am the light, and not only have I told you but I have lived, and you could see it, like a being of light and I have accomplished essential works, I have given back their sight to the blind and I have raised up the dead.

10:26 "but you do not believe,
        because you are not sheep of mine.
10:27 "The sheep that belong to me listen to my voice
        I know them and they follow me,
10:28 "I give them eternal life;
        they will never be lost
        and no one will ever steal them from me."

But you have no faith in the essential because you are not of those whose vital impulse is great. To those who have such an impulse, I can give essential life, eternal truth, since they are receptive to my message; they await it. That is why, having received it, they will no more fall into the danger of death of the soul, of self-banalization.

And he concludes by saying,

10:30 "The Father and I are one."

It must be understood that his works, his entire life, are the manifestation of the essential. This is again the condition for true faith.

Verses 10:33–38 bring the clear and indisputable explanation that Jesus, when he calls himself "Son of God" does not mean to be taken for an actual god.

10:31 The Jews fetched stones to stone him.

10:32 so Jesus said to them: "I have done many good works for you to see, works from my Father; for which of these are you stoning me?"

10:33 The Jews answered him: "We are not stoning you for doing a good work but for blasphemy; you are only a man and you claim to be God."

10:34 Jesus answered:
"Is it not written in your Law:
I said you are gods?"

10:35 "So that the Law uses the word gods,
of those to whom the word of God was addressed,
and Scripture cannot be rejected,

10:36 "Yet to say to someone the Father has consecrated and sent into the world
"You are blaspheming."
Because he says: "I am the Son of God."

10:37 "If I am not doing my Father's work,
there is no need to believe in me.

10:38 "but if I am doing it,
then even if you refuse to believe in me,
at least believe in the work I do;
then you will know for sure
that the Father is in me and I am
in the Father."

There is no need even for commentary. It is quite clear that Jesus says of himself, or at least the Evangelist says about him, that he is a real man, a man like all other men. But all men can be called gods, children of God, if "the word of God is given to them"; i.e., if the Holy Spirit, the spirit of truth animates them.

Jesus himself is animated by the spirit of truth, and by this very fact is a child of God; yet he is more: he is "the only Son" because he is man *par excellence*, the man who justifies all other men in the face of life's meaning, the sanctified man. His works testify that he is fully animated by the Holy Spirit. One must see, through his appearance, "the Essence," one must understand the sanctity of his works, one must lift up the Son of Man in one's soul, one must know that the Son of Man is Son of God. One must know that the mysterious organizing intentionality can be manifested through man to be stimulated to manifest it through oneself. One must have true faith to be reborn, to resurrect, to have essential life, to be justified in the face of the meaning of life.

The dogmatic concept—the foundation of all the erroneous speculation—contradicts not only this passage that gives the only possible definition of the image of God, but also the deep meaning of the whole Gospel. The dogmatic concept of God goes against the evidence of both the appearance and the mystery. For what could be a real God if not something impossible by its very nature? It is neither a really existing reality, nor an image explaining the mystery; it is a pseudoreality belonging neither to the appearance nor to the "Essence." It is a reality outside of existing reality: it is a contradiction in itself. The real God, if he wants to be something else and more than mystery—limit of the human spirit's competence—becomes less than a reality. This anthropomorphic ghost is in fact nothing but the deepest profanation of the mystery called God; it is an exalted love of the ego, disguised as God, deified; it is a vanity of the self, the monster itself, seated on the throne and adored. For there is nothing vainer and emptier than to want a real God concerning himself with this fleeting being that man is, a speck of dust in the vastness of the Cosmos. Nothing is vainer and emptier than to hope that this God could be able actually to resurrect decomposed corpses; this is granting to oneself an importance such that the idea of vanishing forever is quite unacceptable. Psyche and body are inseparable. If one dies, so does the other, since psyche and body are the two aspects of a single phenomenon: the body is the means to achieve the desires that, as feelings of dissatisfaction, are the psychic aspect of the phenomenon. If the body vanishes, the feelings of dissatisfaction and satisfaction that go with the biological functions cease immediately. What does not vanish is the mystery of animation, called *soul*, and which is generally confused with the psyche.[42] This is the confusion of religious dogmatism, and the latter uses the former to maintain belief in the resurrection of the body.

CHAPTER 21

The Glorification

The end of chapter 11 relates the condemnation of Jesus by the Sanhedrin. The order is given for him to be arrested wherever he can be found (see 11:50,53,57).

11:57 The chief priests and the Pharisees had by now given
their orders; anyone who knew where he was must inform them
so that they could arrest him.

Although Jesus knows that death is certain to ensue, he goes to Jerusalem for the coming feast of the Passover. The people, instead of seizing him as the Pharisees had commanded, prepare a triumphal entry for him. In this sense, the people remain opposed to the Pharisees. The latter finally found the solution to the problem Jesus had posed to them. They came to the conclusion that Jesus is a madman.

10:20 Many said: "He is possessed, he is raving; why bother to
listen to him?"

The solution of the crowd is quite different. All their convictions revolve around their messianic delusions. Some of them expect from Jesus the achievement of their delusory hopes; others have ceased hoping in him, he has disappointed them. Those who hope in him are, however, numerous enough to turn his entry in Jerusalem into a public event. A crowd acclaims him: "Hosanna! Blessed is he who comes in the name of the Lord, the king of Israel." Could there be yet another group of people adding to the din of the acclamation only to mock Jesus and the Pharisees who have condemned him? Jesus does not concern himself with this pathetic spectacle that suddenly appears around him; he is not moved. Seated on the colt of a donkey, he goes through the crowd that augurs his unavoidable fate, just as he went through the world without being stained. He has only come because he did not want to run away. No other solution would have been possible (see our explanation of verse 12:31 on page 185).

12:15 "Do not be afraid, Daughter of Zion, see, your king is coming mounted on the colt of a donkey."

12:16 At the time his disciples did not understand this, but later, after Jesus had been glorified, they remembered that this had been written about him, and that this was in fact how they had received him.

As has been shown, reference to the Bible is not proof of a prophecy about Jesus. For instance, in Zachariah,

9:9 "Rejoice heart and soul, daughter of Zion!
. . . See now, your king comes to you;
. . . riding on a donkey,
on a colt, the foal of a donkey."

The colt of a donkey is a symbol of humility. Now, the prophets had always announced the coming of a king according to the spirit. The king was not one who would come in the garb of earthly splendors, but quite to the contrary, in utmost simplicity. Such was, to be sure, the attitude of Jesus. "Do not fear, daughter of Zion, nothing can happen to you if you remain faithful to Yahweh; there will arise from your midst the Messiah who will talk about the 'Eternal one' (the eternal truth)."

This was written. This was foretold, but the prediction concerns the Messiah and not the man Jesus. This is why the Evangelist can say (12:16) that it was accomplished in the person of Jesus, since those who witnessed the moral resurrection of Lazarus spoke about the spiritual royalty of Jesus, about the strength of his spirit, about the true king he is for Jerusalem (see verse 12:17).

12:23 Jesus replied to them:
"Now the hour has come
for the Son of Man to be glorified."

He comes neither to dare the Pharisees to act nor to surrender to them. He who said many times that he did not seek his own glory but that of the one who had sent him, will finally be glorified; the evolutionary spirit that animates every creature and that has been incarnate to the highest degree in the man Jesus, will—thanks to the sublimating strength of that man—be finally glorified. The sublime possibilities will, through the personality of Jesus, blossom to their fullest extent. Up until then his hour "had not yet come," neither historically because the Pharisees had not yet decided to eliminate him, nor essentially because he himself had not yet freed himself from the anxiety of death. But now all is ripe.

> 12:24 "I tell you most solemnly,
>   unless a wheat grain falls on the ground and dies
>   it remains only a single grain;
>   but if it dies,
>   it yields a rich harvest."

For such a sublime blossoming to be achieved, one must accept the total transformation of one's being, accept to die in one form in order to be reborn in another; this image is analogous to that of the phoenix being reborn out of its ashes. It is also connected with the myth of Demeter,[43]

> 12:25 "Anyone who loves his life loses it;
>   anyone who hates his life in this
>   world
>   will keep it for eternal life."

He who loves life in its accidental form, will lose his essential life; anyone who detaches himself from the excessive attraction of this accidental life, will have a taste of essential life.

> 12:26 "If a man serves me, he must follow me,
>   wherever I am, my servant will be there too.
>   If anyone serves me, my Father will honor him."

If anyone wants to serve the ideal that I represent, let him follow my example, not literally, but according to the spirit of what I have taught, let him prefer the essential to the accidental: let him not be led astray by the weight of conventions and the attraction of pleasures. This is what I did, and anyone who does it, will be with me, in the same intentionality; the spirit of life (my Father) will be honored in him, and by this fact, he himself will be honored by the spirit, transfigured by its action.

12:27 "Now my soul is troubled.
What shall I say?
Father, save me from this hour!
But it was for this very reason that I have come to this hour.
12:28 "Father, glorify your name!"

The ultimate hesitation in the face of death is uttered with all the genuineness of a soul that does not lie to itself. This is the simplest confession that can be, the most intense force; the conclusion of the deliberation is supreme acceptance, without regret or accusation, without argument or struggle, a calm victory over worldly disquiet, a humble and unseen inner victory, without demands and without acclaim, without sentimentality and without vanity, the most peaceful and at the same time the most heroic victory, the ultimate achievement of all mythical struggles. This is why he will be able to say later,

16:33 "In the world, you will have trouble,
but be brave;
I have conquered the world."

Now the decisive hour has come, the high point of his mission.

12:28 ". . . A voice came from heaven: "I have glorified it and I will glorify it again."
12:29 People standing by, who heard this, said it was a clap of thunder; others said: "It was an angel speaking to him."

The voice is symbolic. It is the symbol of the deep feeling moving the crowd; faced with the achievement of Jesus, the crowd becomes receptive to his message for a moment, it is swayed by the power of this acceptance. Yet this feeling is more or less confused, more or less intensely lived depending on the vital impulse of each individual. This receptiveness of the crowd was already noted at the beginning of the mission, at the time of the baptism in the Jordan, and it is manifested when the mission is essentially accomplished; at the time of the glorification of human nature and its essential possibilities. Jesus himself explains why in the following verse:

12:30 Jesus answered: "It was not for my sake that this voice came, but for yours."

I have been always animated by a deep awareness of the greatness of human nature, accomplished through my life. But such was not the case for you; yet, in the face of the acceptance that you are witnessing, an acceptance that puts a seal on all I am proposing, you have been moved. You are now moved by this deep feeling.

> 12:31 "Now sentence is being passed on this world;
> now the prince of this world is to be overthrown."

Since this is now the hour when the prince of the world, vanity, "is to be overthrown"—i.e., definitively eliminated from his psyche—when therefore the world is judged (see 18:19), it is thus clear that the time of liberation has come, the time of the world's salvation. The hour of salvation is not the hour of the visibly manifest achievement, but the hour of the inner achievement, the hour of acceptance. Inner acceptance without the outer achievement of the accepted Passion would be incomplete, it could be mistaken for a gesture without proof, but the outer achievement, death suffered, the crucifixion would have no meaning except that of an event occurring many times before and after, if it had not been preceded by the unique, complete and decisive victory over the leader of the world; i.e., that which kills the world, vanity. The latter having been conquered, it can no longer cause anxiety to the victor—victim of this hostile world— because all his energy, all his strength, is concentrated in a single desire, detached from the world and its threats, essential desire. It is because of this essential desire, which animates all men, but has become in him alone the sole reality, the truth lived and manifest, it is because of this essential desire and not because of the crucifixion that he can predict that the souls of all men "will be drawn to him" (see the following verse).

> 12:32 "And when I am lifted up from the earth,
> I shall draw all men to myself."

When the truth lived by Jesus is fully shining, when it is no longer stifled in man's soul by his attachment to earthly desires, when it becomes truth in the spirit of men on the basis of the example he gave, or the words he taught, or on the basis of any veracious formulation—analogous of necessity to the one he proposed—then the truth will draw all men; in the long run, the need for truth is the deepest because it is more satisfying than vanity. The quest for the truth is the essential reality of life, the evolutionary meaning of apparent life, the meaning of its evolution toward the Essence; the history of man is his evolution toward more and more lucidity, because lucidity has proven itself, in the course of the species' evolution, the surest way to obtain satisfaction. Only the evolutionary spirit on its constantly ascending path, will be able, during the course of centuries or even millennia, to understand the hope represented by the example of that man: the tremendous hope of a possible moral resurrection. It will be then that Jesus, through his example, will draw the souls of all men, and awaken in all men the desire to live above all for the essential.

This "miracle" will be achieved by the truth, which quite obviously will be formulated in a different way, although it will remain analogous to the formulation proposed by Jesus. Therefore Jesus is not the one who will draw all men to himself; it will be the Christ, the truth he embodied. Only the formulation evolves, the basis remains the same: to prefer the essential to the accidental. The affirmation that he will draw men, that he will lift their soul, is not a miraculous prophecy but a prediction that is psychologically well founded. It has not yet been fulfilled, and for it to remain veracious, we must introduce the idea of the evolutionary Spirit. It is therefore because of the evolutionary necessity itself that the prediction will be fulfilled.

Given this evolutionary necessity, what are the two thousand years that have followed the life and death of that unique man? The misunderstanding beclouding the signification of this life and death may have driven people to believe that the attraction of experienced truth could be erased little by little, that the essential desire could lose its sway on the human soul.

In this view, it becomes certain that the following verse,

12:33 "By these words, he indicated the kind of death he would die."

is an interpolation and that the words of Jesus (12:32) do not deal with the crucifixion, nor with the quasi-magical power of redemption it is supposed to have. This certainty is confirmed by a careful reading of the passages following this explanation of the elevation. For in verse 12:34, the Jews ask Jesus for an explanation about the elevation he just referred to. But Jesus' explanation is directly opposed to the explanation given in the interpolation. Far from containing any reference to the crucifixion, it clearly reestablishes the essential and genuine meaning of the elevation. The Jews ask,

12:34 "The Law has taught us that the Christ will remain forever. How can you say, 'The Son of Man must be lifted up? Who is this Son of Man?'"

Since the Christ will remain forever and the Pharisees are convinced that they are faithful to the Christ, what then is the business of this Son of Man, and above all what does he mean by "his elevation"?

These are two questions. And what Jesus will say is therefore an answer to both questions. The second question, "who is this Son of Man?" is the usual question of the Pharisees: "Who are you?" Jesus tells them,

12:35 "The light will be with you only a little longer now. Walk while you have the light, or the dark will overtake you; he who walks in the dark does not know where he is going.
12:36 "While you still have the light, believe in the light and you will become sons of light."

Light is the manifestation of the essential, incarnate in a man, expressed by his words and his deeds. Jesus therefore replies to them: "I am the light—follow me—it is as the light that I will draw all men to myself."

And at the same time, Jesus answers their first question: "How can one lift up the Son of Man in himself? One must walk in the light, have faith in the light: i.e., fill oneself with faith in the essential and it is in such a way that you will lift up in your souls the Son of Man, and that you will give him—the incarnate truth—the importance he deserves; this is the elevation of the soul, lifting up the Son of Man in the souls of men, understanding his example and his message; this is moral resurrection, rebirth from symbolic death, awakening from banalization." Thus, when their vital impulse is sufficiently strong, men will become "children of light," sons of "the Essence."

The answer that Jesus gives to the two main questions in the entire Gospel: Who is the Son of Man, and what does the elevation mean, the answer Jesus, before his foreseeable death, gives to the people who represent the entire world, the decisive answer does not say anything therefore, about the lifting up on the cross, it sums up the true condition for salvation: faith in the mysterious intentionality of life, elevation of the soul. Thus, essential desire must not remain theoretical but become active, alive, vivifying, it therefore includes an effort—depending on strength of each individual—to manifest this organizing intentionality through one's activity, the effort to live essentially, to be reborn out of banalization. This active and vivifying understanding is the true faith, sole condition for salvation.

> 12:37 Though they had been present when he gave so many signs,
> they did not believe in him;
> 12:38 this was to fulfill the words of the prophet Isaiah:
> *Lord, who could believe what we have heard said, and to whom has the power of the Lord been revealed?*
> 12:39 Indeed they were unable to believe, because as Isaiah says again;
> 12:40 *He has blinded their eyes, he has hardened their hearts, for fear they should see with their eyes and understand with their hearts, and turn to me for healing.*

As ever, this is not a prophecy fulfilled because it had been made. Since the beginning of time, the manifestations of the organizing spirit, at work in the whole of nature, are here to be seen by men and they do not see them. The prophet Isaiah was able to hear in his inner dialogue with God—symbol of his own superconscious—the voice of the essential and he transmitted it to the Jewish people. But who had faith in what he said? And to whom was immanent justice—joy or suffering, the consequence of justly or unjustly motivated actions—revealed if not to the prophet, the man of God? But does anybody else understand it? And if they did not understand, it is because their eyes were blinded and their hearts hardened.

Blindness and hardening appear (according to the text) as the consequence of a divine intention, but this symbolic expression means only the lawful punishment for error. Yahweh—i.e., immanent justice—metes out the punishment.

If they are blinded, it is because they let themselves become blind by being drawn to the accidental.

12:41 Isaiah said this when he saw his glory, and his words referred
to Jesus.

It was when Isaiah understood the splendor of life and was
dazzled by the immanence of justice that he uttered those words.

12:42 And yet, there were many who did believe in him, even among
the leading men, but they did not admit it, through fear of the
Pharisees and fear of being expelled from the synagogue;
12:43 they put honor from men before the honor that
comes from God.

Just as the Jews of old, blinded by the attraction of pleasures
had been unable to hear the call of the prophet Isaiah. So when
Jesus talks to them, though many Jews feel that this man offers
them the truth, they lack the courage to abandon the promises
of the world and the approval of man.

Verse 12:43 spells out clearly the reason for the essential failure not only of the Jews in Jesus' time, but also of all mankind.
The conventional submission to false social values (material success at all cost, search for honors, desire for consideration) leads
to hatred of the truth. Conventionality of spirit is the greatest
danger that can threaten the world.

The teaching given in verses 12:44–50 is not meant for the
hostile world, but for the faithful disciples. It is a summary of
the preceding discourses and needs no translation.

CHAPTER 22

Washing the Feet

13:1 It was before the festival of the Passover, and Jesus knew that the hour had come from him to pass from this world to the Father. He had always loved those who were his in the world, but now he showed how perfect his love was.

Foreseeing his coming death, Jesus will, in this astonishing act of "washing the feet," show the depth of his love for his disciples.

13:2 They were at supper, and the devil had already put it into the mind of Judas Iscariot, son of Simon, to betray him.

13:3 Jesus knew that the Father had put everything into his hands and that he had come from God, and was returning to God

13:4 and he got up from table, removed his outer garment, and taking a towel, wrapped it around his waist.

While vanity (the devil) had already led Judas to betrayal, Jesus knows that now essential determination is the only one he follows, that he is truly son of "the Essence" and that through death, he returns to "the Essence"; he knows that he is completely freed from any kind of attachment, even the esteem of his disciples. He therefore prepares himself to "wash their feet"— i.e., to purify their soul—since the foot is in symbolic thought (myths and dreams), the symbol of the soul.[44] He removes his outer garment, he therefore gives up any external stance; he unveils the depth of his soul; symbolically speaking: "he bares himself"; he had not done so before because he would not have been understood. He wraps around his waist a towel, symbol of the purity of his intentions and his combative strength, the waist being the locus of physical strength and power, and therefore the symbol of psychic combativeness (see Is 11:15, "Integrity is the loincloth around his waist").

> 13:5 He then poured water into a basin and began to wash the disciples' feet, and to wipe them with the towel he was wearing.

All these gestures symbolize the labor of purification he achieves with his disciples. How does he purify them? By his words and explanations, by the demonstration of their vanity, as we are going to see.

> 13:6 He came to Simon Peter who said to him:
> "Lord, are you going to wash my feet?"

Peter demurs, but since Jesus certainly did not actually wash their feet but showed them their faults, what does this reticence mean on the part of Peter, who always has such good intentions? Verse 9—

> 13:9 ". . . not only my feet, but my hands and my head as well!"
> —shows, on the contrary, that he is quite eager to receive the help of Jesus. We can therefore ask ourselves how Jesus presented the theme to the disciples since Peter, according to the façade of the image, saw Jesus' stooping to purify his soul as some kind of indignity on his part.

What we learn from the knowledge of psychic functioning is that Jesus "having greatly loved his own" (verse 13:1) will go all the way, baring himself to them (verse 13:4) to make them understand the magnitude of human vanity.

He showed them, without being afraid of losing their esteem, but only moved by the desire to help them, the human weakness that he himself, close to perfection as he was, had to overcome. One must not forget the temptation of Jesus narrated by Matthew and Mark: the latter stresses (4:13) that "the devil left him, to return at the appointed time." Obviously the devil is the vain temptation that attacks Jesus in his inner deliberation; it suffices to reread the diabolic offer whispered to him in order to be convinced. It is thus certain that Jesus, a man among other men, had to struggle against vanity, and no one has been better able than he to measure the danger inherent in human nature. He referred to it with the help of metaphorical and parabolic images, but also in a relatively clear way, according to what the evangelist infers (see Lk 12:43). No one has been better able than Jesus to put people on their guard against this danger, or help them overcome it.

How could he have helped his disciples more efficaciously than by showing that he himself had to struggle all his life against vanity? Never had he mastered it more surely than when he openly admitted the force of seduction it exerts on the human psyche. The real difference between Jesus and other men is that he definitively overcame it; which is why he can say,

> 12:31 "Now sentence is passed on this world; now the prince
> of this world is to be overthrown. . . .
> 16:33 "But be brave, I have conquered the world."

This makes him a saint. It is understandable that Peter, in his admiration for Jesus, did not want to admit that the latter was humanly subject to temptation.

All the more so that this reaction is a front for Peter's vanity. Being faced by the weakness—if such we can call it—of Jesus, does he not have now to become aware of the magnitude of his own? Peter follows Jesus, he is devoted to him, eager to understand the essential—his life is exemplary—and yet he has to recognize his essential weakness, which will become so obvious when he will deny Jesus. This is hard to admit. To refuse to admit the fallibility of human nature, manifested in the person of Jesus, is to refuse to recognize the degree of one's own weakness, one's own insufficiency.

This is why Peter, half moved by a real admiration for the Master and half moved by a false motivation, is afraid of being thus made naked, which concerns Jesus as well as himself.

> 13:17 Jesus answered: "At the moment you do not know what I am
> doing, but later you will understand."

You will understand what I am doing when your inner experience makes you face little by little the stubbornness of your vanity and its magnitude.

> 13:8 "Never!," said Peter, "You shall never wash my feet!," Jesus
> replied, "If I do not wash you, you can have nothing in common
> with me."

Peter still does not understand. Which is why Jesus tells him that if he does not want to accept this purification, he will not enter the kingdom of joy. This kingdom of joy is the inner state in which man finds himself when he is no longer under the sway of vanity, of the secret and enormous conceit of believing himself better than all others. Jesus, though, is the "Only Son of God," and what humility must be his to say so and not to attach vanity to this fact! The reality of it makes it true humility, and this reality does not prevent Jesus from showing Peter the bond that unites them in the common human condition.

13:9 "Then Lord," said Simon Peter, "not only my feet but my hands and my head as well!"

Peter has understood; now he wants not only the purification of his soul, his deep intentionality, but also of his activity (hands) and his valuations (head); i.e., he wants his deep emotion to be incarnate, to become a motivation.

13:10 Jesus said: "No one who has taken a bath needs washing, he is clean all over. You too are clean, though not all of you."

One who has washed himself in the truth, who has therefore purified his deep intentionality (feet) need not preoccupy himself with the purification of his behavior (hands), nor of his thoughts (head). He is truly pure. The last sentence refers to Judas.

13:12 When he had washed their feet and put on his clothes again he went back to the table. "Do you understand," he said, "what I have done to you?"

After he has accomplished this unique deepening during which he bared himself before them, he goes back to his usual attitude and asks them if they have understood the scope of what he had just told them.

13:13 "You call me Master and Lord, and rightly. So I am.
13:14 "If I, then, the Lord and Master, have washed your feet, you should wash each other's feet.
13:15 "I have given you an example so that you might copy what I have done to you.
13:16 "I tell you most solemnly: no servant is greater than his master, no messenger is greater than the man who sent him."

I am your Master and you know it. If therefore, I have helped you to purify yourselves by showing you the connection between my faults and yours, you must also know that all of you fall into the same temptations, the same weaknesses and this knowledge will protect you against the notion that one is greater than another. This knowledge will protect you against vain competition.

I have given you the example, not by crushing you with my superiority but by showing you my own weakness. Obviously you are not greater than I am, then do as I have done, confess your faults to one another. It will help you to overcome them.

The proposal to feed them with his body—a symbolic offer—whose explanation was given in the fourth chapter (the multiplication of the loaves, is related by the Synoptic Gospels during the narrative of the Last Supper.

With a quite different symbolic expression, the "washing of the feet," taking place too during the Paschal meal, has the same significance. To feed on the truth, to see the truth about oneself, are one and the same thing.

> 13:18 "I am not speaking about all of you: I know the ones I have chosen; but what scripture says must be fulfilled: '*Someone who shares my table rebels against me.*'"

He goes back to the concept expressed in verse 13:11. Not all of you are capable of taking up this proposal, for one of you, nourished with the word of truth (bread is a symbol of truth), will attempt to destroy me. Again, this is not a prediction in the common sense of the term. The prophets were always able—since they had the experience—that the truth is hard to accept for those whose vital impulse is insufficient; the truth offends, and an offended man seeks revenge. This is so human that it is easy to perceive.

Jesus was a fine psychologist and the motives that animated Judas did not escape him. He himself said, "Jerusalem, you kill your prophets" (see Mt 23:37).

> 13:19 "I tell you this now, before it happens,
> so that when it does happen you may
> believe that I am He."

I warn you in advance, treachery is part of human nature; do not doubt the value of the truth and its convincing force. No matter what happens, keep faith in the hope I represent, even if this hope is betrayed by one of you. Such things are unavoidable and prove nothing against the truth (see 16:33).

As we have already said, the Scriptures are not concerned with Jesus and his accidental fate, but with the Christ, the anointed of the Lord, the one who has been expected since the beginning of time by men of vital impulse, but will always be rejected by the world.

> 13:20 "I tell you most solemnly whoever welcomes the one I send welcomes me, and whoever welcomes me welcomes the one who sent me."

He concludes, you are my disciples and if one listens to your word, he hears mine and my word is essential truth, the truth of the superconscious, the symbolic Father.

The following verses are the clear warning to the disciples of Judas' betrayal. Paul Diel in his book *The God-Symbol*, in the chapter called "The Myth of Redemption," explains this passage. We will give here a summary outline. The one who will betray him

> 13:26 ". . . is the one to whom I give the piece of bread that I shall dip in the dish." He dipped the piece of bread and gave it to Judas son of Simon Iscariot.

Bread and wine (see the Wedding at Cana, the Multiplication of the Loaves) are the spiritualization and sublimation offered to Judas as they were to the others. Bread dipped into wine will have the antithetic significance, a frequent means used in symbolism to convey the link between the sublime and the perverse. The bread reddened by wine becomes the bloody body of Jesus, the consequence of Judas' treachery. Moreover, this symbolism makes it possible to express the forgiveness that Jesus grants Judas by offering him the dipped bread, since the wine, the symbol of sublimation, is the expression of the gift of the soul.

> 13:27 At that instant, after Judas had taken the bread, Satan entered him. Jesus then said, "What you are going to do, do it quickly."

The more forgiveness is offered him and truth given him, the more guilty feelings must be repressed and the more he is filled with the vain certainty that what he does is right. Vain guiltiness is symbolized by Satan. What follows needs no explanation. Likewise, verses 31 to 33—repetitions of verses that have already been translated (see 12:28–29, 7:33, 8:21)–will not be translated.

13:34 "I give you a new commandment: love one
another; just as I have loved you, you must also
love one another.

13:35 "By this love you have for one another everyone
will know that you are my disciples."

This new commandment is love. It is the conclusion of the
whole Gospel. We will return to it in the analysis of chapter 15.

13:36 Simon Peter said, "Lord, where are you going?" Jesus replied:
"Where I am going, you cannot follow me now; you will follow
me later."

13:37 Peter said to him: "Why can't I follow you now? I will lay down
my life for you."

13:38 "Lay down your life for me?", answered Jesus, "I tell you most
solemnly, before the cock crows you will have disowned me
three times."

I am going to die, says Jesus, I am returning to the mystery I
came from (it being understood that this phrase remains symbolic since mystery is neither a space nor a place nor anything
that could exist spatiotemporally).

But Peter is not mature enough to assume death, such as
Jesus has accepted it, in the sublime decision that it is better to
die in the body than to die in the soul. This is why Jesus tells
him, "Where I am going, you cannot follow me." You cannot
follow me in this total acceptance of the situation. Still, he had
enough trust in him to assure him that the time will come; which
was proven true. At this point in time, Jesus, who knows human
weakness, can assure him that confronted by the world and the
pressure it can exert, Peter will be led to deny him because of his
anxiety of other's opinion and anxiety for his own life.

CHAPTER 23

The Paraclete

In the following chapters, most verses are now understandable. This is why they will not all be quoted.

> 14:2 "There are many rooms in my Father's house;
> if there were not, I should have told you.
> 14:3 "I am going now to prepare a place for you
> and after I have gone and prepared you a place,
> I shall return to take you with me;
> so that where I am
> you may be too.
> 14:4 "You know the way to the place where I am going."

The first part of verse 2 has already been translated.

If only the saint could live in the essential, I would have told you so, but each one of you will get his reward, his joy, in accordance with the vital impulse he has. When, through my teaching and my example, and in particular the example of my acceptance of the death I am going to suffer, I will have prepared you to understand the meaning of life, when time has enabled you to evolve in the direction I took, then you will always be with me since you will live in the dimension where I have lived.

Now you know the way to the essential. After having told them several times (see 13:33), "Where I am going you cannot come," Jesus feels now that his disciples are more capable of understanding.

Yet, when Philip tells him,

> 14:8 "Lord, let us see the Father and we shall be satisfied,"

he finds himself compelled to repeat, once again (see 10:30, 10:38, and 14:9) that he and his Father are a single person; i.e., that he is fully animated by the superconscious; or, again, that it is the Father, the superconscious and only the superconscious, who speaks in him (see 8:28). His inner being is not split between a subconscious and a superconscious, between Satan and God. If the disciples do not understand this, let them at least have faith in him because of the works he has performed in their presence: the blind who see, the dead who rise, etc.

> 14:12 "I tell you most solemnly
> whoever believes in me
> will perform the same works as I do myself,
> he will perform even greater works,
> because I am going to the Father."

Whoever believes in me—i.e., in essential life and the joy it brings—will also act in conformity with the superconscious demands. The ending of the verse is clearly an interpolation because the fact that Jesus goes back to Father—i.e., dies—can in no way enable his disciples to become saints. Dogmatism interprets this as the real help that Jesus can obtain from a real God.

> 14:13 "Whatever you ask in my name I will do,
> so that the Father may be glorified in the Son.
> 14:14 "If you ask for anything in my name
> I will do it."

All that the disciples ask in a spirit of justice and truth, in the spirit of what Jesus taught them, will be given to them because they will not seek the "glory that comes from men, but the glory of God"; they will seek essential satisfaction, which is always accessible because it is acceptance, whatever the accidental givens of life may be.

> 14:16 "I shall ask the Father,
> and he will give you another Advocate [Paraclete]
> to be with you forever,
> 14:17 "that spirit of truth,
> whom the world can never receive,
> since it neither sees nor knows him.
> But you know him
> because he is with you, he is in you."

Paraclete means "advocate." Thus, this other advocate who will be with them forever is the spirit of truth, it is the reference to truth. Truth exists, it is the truth about the *meaning* of life, therefore about its direction that is evolutionary and about its significance that is joy insofar as evolution toward more and more lucidity is assumed; truth is, because of this, truth about the hidden intentions that each one of us is fostering in his inner self. The acknowledgment of these repressed motives enables them to be dissolved. Once such a capacity has been acquired, no outside help is needed.

Verse 14:26 states this clearly:

> "But the Advocate, the Holy Spirit,
> whom my Father will send in my name,
> will teach you everything
> and remind you of all I have said to you."

But this spirit of truth, this quest for the truth about oneself, about one's weaknesses, not in words and in inner confession but in an avowal that can profoundly transform the being, is not accepted by the world. They, however, will receive the "Paraclete," they will develop this lucidity about themselves that was offered to them by Jesus, because they have experienced the tremendous satisfaction, the joy, that it brings.

> 14:18 "I will not leave you orphans;
> I will come back to you.
> 14:19 "In a short time, the world will no longer see me,
> but you will see me
> because I live and you will live.
> 14:20 "On that day,
> you will understand that I am in my Father
> and you in me and I in you."

The world will not see him anymore because he will be dead. He will not come back in the body, contrary to what the dogma of the Resurrection claims. But the spirit of truth that animated him from the beginning and that he transmitted to his disciples will animate them, when the shock of his death, which will leave them in a state of disorientation for a while, is overcome; what will make him an eternally living being is the truth that he has incarnated, the Christ, who will never die.

This resurrection of Christ is directly connected to the moral resurrection, for each time a man lives according to the truth, the spirit of truth that animated Jesus, Christ, is alive again. This is why the disciples will also be "alive," they will have escaped essential death. It is then that they will understand the true relationship between the Father and the Son, the essential desire fully animating the Son and the genuine relationship between the Son and his disciples: union in essential desire.

> 14:22 Judas—this was not Judas Iscariot—said to him: "Lord, what is this all about? Do you intend to show yourself to us and not to the world?"
> 14:23 Jesus replied:
> "If anyone loves me he will keep my word
> and my Father will love him,
> and we shall come to him
> and make our home with him."

The disciples are the only ones who will understand. The point is not that he does not want to show himself to the world, but that the world does not want him. He reveals himself to all those who are capable of receiving his message. It is enough to love truth more than vanity, and to receive it in one's soul in order to become the "Son of the Father," one whose vital impulse is brought back to life.

We will translate here several verses from chapter 16:

> 16:7 "Still, I must tell you the truth:
> it is for your own good that I am going
> because unless I go,
> the Advocate will not come to you;
> but if I do go,
> I will send him to you."

It is good for me to go because, only when you find yourselves alone, without my help, will you become aware that, if you want to go on in the way you have chosen, you have to muster all your strength in order truly to understand what I proposed to you. Were I to remain with you, you would continue to rely on me and you would not attempt to assume by yourselves the spirit of truth. When you are alone in the face of the world, your faith will be tried: either you will abandon everything, but this is hardly possible since guiltiness would overwhelm you; or you will have to find certainty. My death can thus be for you a source of deepening.

> 16:8 "And when he comes,
> he will show the world how wrong it was,
> about sin,
> and about who was in the right,
> and about judgment:
> 16:9 "about sin:
> proved by their refusal to believe in me
> 16:10 "about who was in the right:
> proved by my going to the Father
> and your seeing me no more;
> 16:11 "about judgment:
> proved by the prince of this world being already condemned."

Having no faith in "the Essence," the world commits the sin against the spirit of truth, the only sin that will not be forgiven (see page 109).

Justice will be manifested, since what awaits me is a return to the Father-Essence, and this is just, because I lived in the essential.

Faced with the truth, the error of the world becomes quite overwhelming; faced with the manifestation of the "Essence," the error of vanity (the leader of this world) is obvious. Its judgment is the essential dissatisfaction it provides.

The following verses have already been explained: we refer the reader to the translation of verses 14, 17, 18, and 19. Now it is clearly said,

> 16:13 "But when the spirit of truth comes
> he will lead you to the complete truth,
> since he will not be speaking as from himself
> but will say only what he has learned;
> and will tell you of things to come."

Verses 16:16–23 develop the same theme: the second coming of Christ, of the Holy Spirit and not of Jesus, to them; i.e., the wonderful moment when:

> 16:22 ". . . your hearts will be full of joy
> and that joy no one shall take from
> you.

> 16:23 "When that day comes,
> you will not ask me any
> questions."

On that day, they will have nothing more to ask from this man who, until then, had given them the key to the truth since they have in themselves the possibility of finding the solution to the problem of life, the strength to take it upon themselves be it until death.

It is at the end of chapter 16, verses 25 to 33, that Jesus grants his disciples a sufficient understanding and no longer talks in the form of parables. And his disciples tell him, "Now you are speaking plainly"; matured by trial and having been taught daily by Jesus, they have little by little opened to the essential dimension proposed to them.

In chapter 15, verse 15, did he not tell them that they have now become his friends since he has given them all that his superconscious (the Father) taught him? Now they live in certainty (see 16:30).

Yet Jesus knows their weakness and takes it into account; they will abandon him temporarily, as Peter did; but Jesus finds the thought that will reconcile him with the extremely tragic situation in which he finds himself; even if he is abandoned by his disciples, he will not "be alone" for the Father "is with him" (see 17:21): the superconscious that knows clearly what to tell each individual what has to be done in order to attain satisfaction. Forgetting his own suffering, he goes back to them; they too will suffer (see 16:33):

> "In the world you will have trouble,
> but be brave:
> I have conquered the world."

This is the supreme reality, the supreme consolation, the supreme hope: victory over the world and its prince (vanity in all its forms). This is the comforting conclusion; the struggle he has fought will not have been in vain, it has led to victory.

The end of chapter 14, to which we come back, is very moving.

> 14:27 "Peace I bequeath to you,
> my own peace I give you,

> a peace the world cannot give, this is my gift to you.
> Do not let your hearts be troubled or afraid."

This is the proof that the man Jesus, at the very moment when his death is a certainty, finds himself completely at peace. His greatest desire is to be able to transmit this peace to his disciples. He contrasts it with the "peace of the world" based on the repression of essential guiltiness. Everyone seeks to obtain the tacit complicity of his peers, no matter what he does, and in exchange he implicitly gives them the same indulgence. But this indulgence of compromise is what leads the world to its doom. Sooner or later this "peace," rooted in a general submission to the powers that be, turns into destructive aggressiveness in the form of rebellions, revolutions, or wars.

> 14:29 "I have told this now before it happens,
>   so that when it does happen you may believe."

He tells them what will happen to him (see 13:19) and what they will have to do when they are left alone (all of chapter 14). If they do so, they will develop their faith in the essential.

> 14:30 "I shall not talk with you any longer,
>   because the prince of this world is on his way.
>   He has no power over me.
> 14:31 "but the world must be brought to know that I love the Father
>   and that I am doing exactly what the Father told me."

The prince of this world is coming, and Jesus is his victim. The vanity of the world can only kill his body, but cannot touch his heart nor his courage. He will not sink into complaints nor hateful revenge, and because of this the world will know that he has fully accepted the demands of the superconscious: reconciliation with the world that is killing him and acceptance of death in the joy of victory.

In fact, it was only the Evangelist who could say so, in Jesus' name, a century later; since, shortly before his death, Jesus could not foresee that his message would be heard and understood, at least during the very first centuries of our era.

The beginning of chapter 15 is an allegory that is easy to understand. Let us only stress verse 7, which must be linked with 14:13:

15:7 "If you remain in me and my words remain in you,
you may ask what you will,
and you shall get it."

"To remain in him (Jesus)" means "to keep up the essential search." Then essential satisfaction is always possible, since it is independent of accidental events. It is enough to accept the unchangeable and to change the changeable sensibly in order not to find oneself in the ridiculous situation of wanting what life cannot give.

Verses 9 to 17 of chapter 15 go back to verses 34 and 35 of chapter 13, and develop them.

15:9 "As the Father has loved me,
so I have loved you.
Remain in my love
15:10 "If you keep my commandments,
you will remain in my love,
just as I have kept my Father's commandments
and remain in his love.
15:11 "I have told you this
so that my own joy may be in you
and your joy be complete
15:12 "This is my commandment:
love one another
as I have loved you
15:13 "A man can have no greater love
than to lay down his life for his friends
15:14 "You are my friends
if you do what I command you
15:15 "I shall not call you servants any more,
because a servant does not know
his master's business;
I call you friends,
because I have made known to you
everything I have learned from my Father.
15:16 "You did not choose me,
no, I chose you,
and I commissioned you
to go out and to bear fruit,
fruit that will last,
and then the Father will give you
anything you ask him in my name.

> 15:17 "What I command you
> is to love one another."

Understanding the essential dimension of life leads necessarily, on the plane of the feelings, to what rounds out lucidity of spirit: the sublimation of affectivity.

Love one another, as I have loved you, he tells them; this is objective love, the essential bond that—without any exclusion—links man to other men through the essential desire they all share; it is the possible communication between men in the Essence and through the Essence. Only love of the essential and the joy it brings with it can enable man to rise above pettiness and offenses, jealousies and greed, rancors and sentimentalities.

"Love one another, as I have loved you." This man Jesus knew how to love, and his love was able to perceive the essential man hidden under the accidental man. He relied on the superconscious vital impulse (the Father) that every person has in himself. With this consistent attitude, he manifested his love to those who were with him: he revealed them to themselves.

Thus love is the ultimate achievement of lucidity and its reward. Love is lucidity about life, its meaning, its dimension, it is lucidity about human beings, their possibilities, their sufferings, their abysses and their summits; it is victory over vain egocentrism. Only love enables man to be reconciled with his own natural shortcomings.

In the first epistle of John, we find the same formulations; love is the core of the apostle's teaching (see 3:18 and 4:7–20).

Verse 11 of chapter 15 deserves special attention (see also 17:13):

> 15:11 "I have told you this
> so that my own joy may be in you
> and your joy be complete."

Just as he wanted to transmit to them the peace that was his (14:27), the definitive delivery from anxiety, so he wants to transmit to them his joy, the fullness of his love for life, at the very moment when he knows that the hatred of the world will be unleashed against him. This joy is the most obvious proof that Jesus has freed himself totally from the accidental, even in the face of mortal threats. Even for an ordinary man, the events of

the outer world are not the true determining factors of his psychic state. What determines his joy or his anxiety is the positive or
negative way he reacts to the external event. But it is obvious
that the smaller his vital impulse is, the more man remains subject to external determinations.

Verses 18 to 27 of chapter 15, 1 to 4 of chapter 16 deal with
the hatred of the world for the essential, therefore for Jesus and
his disciples (see 17:14 translated in the following chapter). Nothing can be expected from the world, and one must know this.
Yet, the world is unforgivable because it has been taught.

> 15:22 "If I had not come,
>   if I had not spoken to them,
>   they would have been blameless;
>   but as it is they have no excuse for their sin.
> 15:23 "Anyone who hates me hates my Father."

Thus there is nothing to hope from the world, which is why
he comforts them by saying,

> 16:33 ". . . In the world you will have trouble
>   but be brave,
>   I have conquered the world."

CHAPTER 24

Immanent Justice

Chapter 17 is clarified by the preceding analyses. Only a few verses need stressing:

> 17:2 ". . . and through the power over all mankind that you have given him, let him give eternal life to all those you have entrusted to him.
> 17:3 "And eternal life is this:
> to know you,
> the only true God,
> and Jesus Christ whom you have sent."

Eternal life is not life after death, it is the eternal truth or knowledge of "God," the understanding that "God" is a name for the mysterious organization of the whole of nature. "The one who was sent" by this mystery of the organization is the Christ, the truth lived by the man Jesus who became the anointed of the Lord, it is the clearest, the most highly organized manifestation of the mystery of organization in the form of a human thought. The issue is to know "God" and "Christ" during this life. The power that Jesus has on all mankind—i.e., over all human beings whose vital impulse is sufficiently strong—is to transmit the truth about the meaning of life and to become for them the Christ, the truth incarnate.

> 17:5 "Now, Father, it is time for you to glorify me
> with that glory I had with you
> before ever the world was."

(See verse 24.)

The glory credited to Christ, before the world ever was, is a symbolic image. The harmonious organization of the sanctified man is explicitly present in the first cell, the first crystal, the first atom, all the "organisms"—as the word itself indicates—having existed only in harmonious organization. The sanctified man, incarnation of Christ, draws his glory from the harmony that was preexistent to him, and his organizing power is implicit in the mystery since the mystery "contains" all the appearance. We use the verb "to contain," but it must be repeated, that this is only an image used to evoke this problem since we cannot have the slightest idea about the mystery itself. This is why symbolic expression is the most adequate way of talking about it, when it is understood emotionally and not logically.

> 17:9 "I pray for them;
> I am not praying for the world
> but for those you have given me
> because they belong to you."

The men that God has given him are the men of strong vital impulse, capable of preferring essential life to accidental pleasures. Several times (see 17:11–21,23), Jesus wishes his disciples to attain this unity with the Father, with the superconscious, that he has achieved; it is common union in essential desire.

While "remaining in the world" (see 17:11) because they are not yet threatened by death and they will never be the achievement of the ideal as Jesus was—i.e., completely freed from any attachment to the world—"they are not of this world" (17:14) because their goal is not the accidental pursuits, material success, a quest for the approval of the world (see 15:18–19)

> 17:19 "and for their sake I consecrate myself
> so they too may be consecrated in
> truth."

He prefers to die in the body than in the soul, and this sacrifice of his life, undertaken for his greater joy, is also done for the joy of his disciples, so that immanent justice may become an evidence to them. How could it not be obvious, with such an example, that joy is the just reward of a sublime deliberation?

Far more magnificent than the imagination of a real, ghostly God haunting the psyches impoverished by convention is the vivifying, reconciling idea of a justice that is immanent in the psychic functioning, a justice that is so precise that not one thought, not one feeling can escape from its law. "Every hair on your head has been counted" (Lk 12:7). The slightest thought is a source of satisfaction or dissatisfaction, according to whether it is right or false. Man, in the last analysis, is fully responsible for his slightest thought. How could Jesus, who was so deeply convinced of this, not have wanted to transmit this evidence to his disciples?

Even his death was experienced with joy, in spite of the short moments of anxiety, because it was for him the certainty that, thanks to his disappearance, his disciples would be able to assume the truth.

16:7 ". . . It is for your own good that I am going."

CHAPTER 25

The Kingdom

The most important part of chapter 18 is the conversation between Pilate and Jesus.

To Pilate, who questions him, he clearly says,

> 18:36 "Mine is not a kingdom of this world."

which was understood as meaning "my kingdom in the beyond."

Now, this "world" is the world of banalization in which Pilate lives. As the whole Gospel shows, the kingdom of Jesus is the kingdom of the inner world, the world of joy and suffering, over which he rules because no one has overcome suffering and reached the summit of joy better than Jesus.

Yet he is a king (as he affirms in verse 18:37), the true royalty being that of the spirit in quest of the truth:

> 18:37 "So you are a king then?" said Pilate,
> "It is you who say it," answered Jesus. "Yes, I am a king.
> I was born for this, I came into the world for this: to bear
> witness to the truth; and all who are on the side of truth
> listen to my voice."

To which Pilate, with the skepticism that characterizes decadent eras, shrugs his shoulders, exclaiming "Truth . . . what is that?" Meaning "as if truth existed, as if one could talk about it!"

This is why, when Pilate (19:9), who is however somewhat troubled, having heard that Jesus calls himself the Son of God, asks him, "Who are you?" Jesus does not answer. If the Jews, who had been prepared by the whole Bible to understand the significance of this metaphor (see particularly Jn 10:34 and Ps 82:6), did not understand (because they did not want to understand) how could a Roman of the decadent era understand him?

The following verses relate the death of Jesus.

There is nothing to add except to stress verse 19:24, which quotes Ps 22:19 to claim that it was a prophecy of the most minute details surrounding the death of Jesus. As we have already stressed (page 87), this is not a prediction, but a complaint about the situation, uttered by the just man who has faith in God and is surrounded by "a pack of evil doers" (Ps 22:17) who "mock him because he trusted in Yahweh" (Ps 20:8–9).

Nothing in this passage refers to the future man who will be called Jesus; but the complaint of the "just" man who is rejected by the world is valid for the man Jesus as well as for any other just man in the past and the future; with one difference, however—Jesus never complained about the world but was fully reconciled with it: "Forgive them, they do not know what they are doing" (Lk 23:34).

What had been prophesized was therefore the fate kept in store for the just man, but not the sublime way in which the man of God, who happened to be Jesus, accepted without complaint or reproach the fate that was his. The verse we quoted earlier (Lk 23:34) does not therefore mean, contrary to what dogma claims, that people did kill, without wanting to know it, the real Son of the real God.

In this verse, the Evangelist reveals his deep knowledge of the psychic functioning: blinded by his subconscious vanity, man wants to ignore the motivations that make him act; he even ends up not knowing that within him are very false justifications of his errors. Confronted with the truth incarnate in Jesus, men, who are universally inclined to repress their essential shortcomings, do not know the harm they do to themselves nor that they cause to others by refusing to hear the truth about their motivations. This is the true significance of this verse in which lucidity and acceptance, spiritualization and sublimation, complete one another to express the acme of the human soul.

Chapters 14, 15, 16, and 17 have a greatness and beauty one can penetrate little by little by rereading them many times and by understanding their real meaning.

This man is surrendering his very soul to us; his trust in human nature, his combative enthusiasm, his love for his "brothers," his faith in the essential, his simplicity, his strength, and his joy.

These chapters are poems of love and songs of hope. It is difficult to translate into conceptual language the density and the emotion that symbolic language is capable of expressing.

CHAPTER 26

The Resurrection

Chapters 20 and 21 (like Mt 28, Mk 6, and Lk 24) are narratives that are considered as a faithful report of the bodily resurrection of Jesus.

Added to the Gospel of John, these chapters are not the expression of a genuine symbolic vision, even if symbolic elements are still found in them; for instance, the Ascension. We will come back to this in the following pages. On the plane of textual criticism, it is admitted that chapter 21 is an addition.

These narratives are nothing but a legend, the expression of an age-old hope coming from animism that had a belief in survival after death (animistic belief had a deep significance and the survival of the body was a direct consequence of the primitive vision.[45] This hope, in spite of the evolution of mythical thought that became capable of going beyond animistic realism, remained rooted in the magical layer of the human psyche.

In its symbolic significance, the resurrection is, as we have seen, a fundamental given of the Gospel, but there arose a great confusion in connection with the term. Legend rested on a promise that Jesus himself made to his disciples. This purely symbolic promise, whose significance was outlined on page 199, was understood literally and, to support its claims, legend endeavored to give many concrete details—for instance, John 20:6–7—details that cannot be incorporated in a symbolic translation.

The promised resurrection (referred to in Mt 20:17–19, 10:32–34, Lk 18:31–33) is the resurrection of "Christ" and not of Jesus.

The third day is the day marked by the Spirit, symbolized by the number 3; on that day, the truth that is lived by the man Jesus and that is the eternal truth, will rise from the tomb of oblivion where centuries of misunderstanding and dogmatism have buried it.

Jesus was able to predict this resurrection of the truth, because since the beginning of the world, truth has been struggling to survive; in spite of the errors that are always attempting to destroy it, it emerges victoriously from the tomb; in the long run, truth is more satisfactory than error. It is an expression of harmony, the necessary condition for existence.

This prediction was the expression of the certainty that the world could not live without regaining, sooner or later, the truth taught by Christ, even if that truth were to take thousands of years to be rediscovered, to be formulated anew. He who has experienced the truth and its joy cannot doubt its existence nor its periodic rebirth. He knows that the search for the truth is an evolutionary demand, because it is linked to the progressive acquisition of lucidity and thus to a greater promise of satisfaction.

However, before the full understanding of the truth about the meaning of life—which might require perhaps centuries or thousands of years of evolution—"Christ rises again" each time a human spirit understands the evolutionary demand of life, its immanent truth, and assumes it. On that day the lucid spirit manifests itself in man, his vision is enlightened, the meaning of life, the primacy of the essential over the accidental, are revealed to him; on that day, the eternal truth of all the myths, the truth that was incarnate in the man Jesus, is reborn, brought back to life.

There are thus several significances to the word *resurrection*; it can mean the metaphysical resurrection after the death of the body, a symbolic image meaning simply the return to the "mystery" whence man came (see page 163). It can mean the moral resurrection; i.e., the inner resurgence of man during his lifetime, a resurrection that has been analyzed throughout this translation.

It can mean the resurrection of "Christ"; i.e., the resurgence of the truth struggling against error. This latter form of resurrection is thus linked to the moral resurrection of man during his lifetime since, through his "rebirth" to the life of the spirit—another symbolic expression—man brings truth to the fore, he enables "Christ to rise again."

Some verses in these chapters retain a symbolic content, symbolism having been incorporated into legend. Thus, verse 22 of chapter 20 is a reference to the "descent of the Holy Spirit," achieved as Jesus had predicted it (see the verse: "It is good for you that I am going") when the emotion of the disciples faced with the departure of their Master finally opens their understanding to what he had taught them.

In the same vein, 20:17 is a reference to the Ascension, whose significance is symbolic. Jesus "went back up to heaven" from whence "he had come down." Through death, he has been freed from all the dissatisfactions, of which the greatest had been the misunderstanding of his message. Freed from dissatisfaction, he is back "in the heaven of definitive joy"; of course, this is only an image: every man returns to the essence, but since the psyche of Jesus was completely purified and had become the achievement of the mystery of his animation, the myth expresses this by specifying that not only did his soul go back to the mysterious essence, to "the Father," but also his incarnate soul, symbolized by his body whose manifestations (desires, thoughts, volitions) had all become the very expression of his soul-Essence. This is simply a symbolic and image-laden manner of expressing the difference between the man Jesus and other men. To this significance we must add the one already given on page 161.

The authenticity of the Scriptures is not made questionable by the addition of chapters 20 and 21. For the psychological explanation is based on the rigorous knowledge of symbolic language; when the text cannot be understood symbolically, it can be suspected. Is it not surprising, though, that through the misunderstanding of the centuries, the symbolic narrative did reach us, sufficiently genuine to be translatable in a coherent way? The truth is so powerful, it builds such a coherent structure, that it can be reconstituted in its unity and strength in spite of the excessively good intentions of the copiers who twisted or added certain verses. In the history formed by the texts, the mythical element is the core and the historical facts are the shell. One must not be afraid of discarding the shell; i.e., to distrust the narrative when the unity of the myth is perturbed.

The Christian myth is a "revelation of God," as is any other myth. But the divine revelation itself is a myth that has to be understood. It is the superconscious, the divine in man symbolized by the Father, who "reveals" to the man of strong vital impulse what he must do to find satisfaction. Having understood this, Jesus, in his turn, revealed it to other men, he showed them the immanence of justice, and the possibility of becoming independent of external and accidental events. He brought them the Good News: the possibility of being reborn, during life, from the death of the soul. All this was fully assumed by Jesus himself.

CHAPTER 27

Conclusion

Having been thus translated according to its essential significance, the Gospel of John appears clearly as nothing but a detailed explanation—although one that is written in symbolic language—of the myths formulated and narrated by Jesus himself and also told in the other Gospels: the myths of the incarnation, the redemption, and the resurrection. These myths are implicitly contained in the two phrases used by Jesus in all the Gospels: Son of Man and Son of God.

The work to be done by the man who is animated by true faith is made up of goodness and truth, the opposites of hatred and error, which are the stigmata of the perverted world ruled by its prince, exalted imagination, exalted desires, the monster that the mythical hero must fight; this monster is symbolized in the Christian myth by Satan, it is symbolized in the Greek myth by Medusa, the Chimera, and many other images. The task to be accomplished is therefore the sublimation and spiritualization of desires, the two highest manifestations of the organizing spirit. Now sublimation and spiritualization are—as we have shown—the hidden meaning of all the symbolic struggles of the ancient myths: the goal that was shared by all the ancient heroes of the pagan myths. The pagan myths and the Christian myth testify to the truth that is shared by all cultural eras. This fundamental unity, more or less hidden, of the entire mythical life, shows that the deities of the ancient myths already had the only veracious significance that the symbol of the creative divinity can have: that of "the Essence," the mystery, the mysterious dimension of life, in the face of which the accidental preoccupations lose their importance.

The message of joy brought by Perseus, the victorious hero of the Greek myth, and the message of joy brought by Jesus can be seen as parallels.[46] This message of joy is victory over vanity; the root of vanity is the oblivion of the essential and the vain proposal of seeking one's satisfaction in material and sexual pleasures alone.

The only hope that the Gospel repeatedly expresses is the return to the essential, love of the essential, source of an uncontestable satisfaction because it is independent of the accidents coming from the outer world. The message of joy, the good news brought by Jesus, can be summed up as follows: "Have faith in the organizing intentionality that is immanent in the psyche, and whose reality you can now understand better through my example and words. Become also 'sons of the Father,' be born of the superconscious spirit and you will know what the essential is, the source of all life. Understand that we are judged by the essential demand that we carry in ourselves, and that testifies to all that I propose to you. Essential life develops from the spiritualization-sublimation of exalted desires; this is the food of the soul, symbolized by the flesh of the Son of Man.

Whoever keeps my words, who lives according to my teaching, will never fall into the death of the soul, the oblivion of life's meaning.

Unite yourselves to "the Essence" (the Father) as I did, you will receive the revelation of the truth (the Paraclete) and will thus possess the fullness of joy, since you will be assured that you "will return to the unfathomable mystery."

Do not be afraid of anything since "the spirit of truth" will testify on my behalf (see 15:26); the spirit of truth, the Hope that lives in mankind all through the centuries, the Son, third person of the trinity, will pursue its evolutionary effort toward more and more lucidity.[47]

Through its ever renewed conquests, the spirit of truth will show that Jesus, a man among men, had understood and fully assumed the essential dimension of life, its meaning.

One can ask, at the threshold of the third millennium, when the world is threatened with destruction, if it is still right to have faith in the meaning of life? If mankind is unworthy of living, if it rejects the truth about life and its meaning, it will go to its death; this will only be the manifestation of the immanence of justice. It is yet another way—however tragic it be—to testify to the spirit of truth.

But, having read the Gospel, it does not seem fit to despair of mankind. It is certainly threatened; but in the face of the clear danger will it not be capable of rising to the level demanded by the factual givens of reality? What is certain, no matter what fate awaits mankind, is that only the spirit of truth is a source of satisfaction, of joy, and of life.

The new evolutionary stage, the capacity lucidly to perceive the motivations of one's actions without distorting them through vain anxiety, without projecting them onto the world in sentimental accusation, is becoming nowadays for man, a necessity in the search for satisfaction.

In the scientific era in which we live, the science of the inner world, the only one that could put a stop to the bad use of the science of the outer world, must be able to bring about a methodology of thought able to heal the psyche overstretched by the exaltation of desires, fed by modern technology straying from its goal. The response of man to the mystery of creation will be the work—not only superconscious but also conscious—of spiritualization and sublimation, genuine creation of self by self, called in the Christian myth—the resurrection.

Notes

1. See Paul Diel. The God-Symbol, trans. Nelly Marans (San Francisco: Harper & Row, 1986).
2. Diel, *The God-Symbol*.
3. Paul Diel, *La Psychologie de la Motivation*, Petite Bibliothéque Payot.
4. J. Solotareff, *Le Symbolisme dans les Rêves. La Méthode de Traduction de Paul Diel*, Payot.
5. Paul Diel, *Symbolism in Greek Mythology* trans. Vincent Stuart, Micheline Stuart, Rebecca Folkman (Boston: Shambhala, 1980). and Paul Diel, *Symbolism in the Bible*, trans. Nelly Marans (San Francisco: Harper & Row, 1986).
6. Paul Diel, *La Peur et l'Angoisse*, Petite Bibliothéque Payot.
7. See Diel, *Symbolism in Greek Mythology*.
8. As is well known, the fish was the secret symbol of the early Christians who used the letters of *Ichthus*, the Greek word for fish, as the first letters of each word in the phrase *Iesus CHristus THeo Uios Soter*. That is; "*Jesus Christ, Son of God*, Savior." As is always the case, the symbolic meaning is fundamental, the play on words is secondary.
9. Diel, *Symbolism in Greek Mythology*.
10. Diel, *Symbolism in the Bible*.
11. Diel, *Symbolism in the Bible*.
12. Diel, *Symbolism in Greek Mythology*.
13. For more details, see Diel, *The God-Symbol*.
14. For the sake of easy reference, the traditional numbering of the verses has been retained.
15. The French translation of Osty, used by the author, even though it is influenced by dogmatism, is interesting from the linguistic viewpoint. It points out quite rightly that in the Prologue, the verb *to be* is used exclusively for the Logos (and also for Life, Light; i.e., for essence) while the verbs *to appear* or *to become* concern the appearance or existing world.
16. Diel, *La Psychologie de la Motivation*, Introduction and Chapter I.
17. See Diel, *La Peur et l'Angoisse*.
18. Verses 6, 7, 8, and 9 will be analyzed after verse 18.
19. See p. 5.
20. For an explanation of this term, see Diel, *Symbolism in the Bible*.
21. Diel, *La Peur et l'Angoisse*.
22. On the linguistic plane, the usual translation, "The Word *was made flesh*," now given up by many translators, unduly stretches the meaning of the Greek verb that only means "became" or "has become." Verse 14 does not denote any per-

sonal intention, it describes the incarnation as an evolutionary stage. Small errors of this type are not infrequent in biblical translations. Introduced under the influence of dogmatism, often without conscious awareness on the part of the translator, who based himself on the tradition, they contribute to a perpetuation of belief at the expense of symbolic understanding

23. The same remark applies to the Epistles of Paul.
24. The phrase "Only Son" is found only—and quite rarely at that—in the Gospel of John.
25. The Greek word *simeion*, wrongly translated as "miracle," means simply "sign" and does not introduce any supernatural connotation. The "miracles"of Jesus, like any mythical illogicality, must be interpreted symbolically.
26. Verse 15 will be analyzed after verses 6, 7, 8, and 9 and after the Prologue.
27. The title of the Greek Bible, *Kaine diatheke*, usually translated as "New Testament" can also be translated as "New Covenant."
28. The original text literally says, "the Only Son was his interpreter, was the one who explained his intentions."
29. See Diel, *La Peur et l'Angoisse*.
30. Diel, *Symbolism in the Bible*.
31. It is already found in Babylonian mythology.
32. See the translation of the Prologue in this book and in Diel, *The God-Symbol*, in the chapter on the myth of the trinitarian divinity.
33. Diel, *The God-Symbol*, on the myth of redemption.
34. Solotareff, *Le Symbolisme dans les Rêves*.
35. Solotareff, *Le Symbolisme dans les Rêves*.
36. Diel, *La Psychologie de la Motivation*.
37. Diel, *Symbolism in the Bible*.
38. Diel, *Symbolism in the Bible*, chapter I, Part II.
39. Diel, *Symbolism in the Bible*.
40. Diel, *The God-Symbol*, and *Symbolism in the Bible*.
41. Diel, *Symbolism in the Bible*.
42. See Diel, *The God-Symbol*, chapter entitled "Soul and Psyche."
43. See Diel, *Symbolism in Greek Mythology*
44. See the Introduction.
45. See Diel, *The God-Symbol* and *Symbolism in the Bible*.
46. Diel, *Symbolism in the Bible*.
47. Diel, *The God-Symbol*.